A Rich Poor Life

A Rich Poor Life

Marie Margis

LIFE RATTLE PRESS   TORONTO, CANADA

A Rich Poor Life

Marie Margis

Second Edition

Published by Life Rattle Press, Toronto, Canada

Copyright © 2013 by Marie Margis

Library and Archives Canada Cataloguing in Publication

Margis, Marie, 1941-, author
A rich poor life / Marie Margis.

(New writers series)
ISBN 978-1-927023-81-5 (pbk.)

I. Title. II. Series: Life Rattle new writers series

PS8626.A7495R43 2013   C813'.6   C2013-905166-X

Edited by: John Dunford

All photographs courtesy of the author

Cover design and typeset by: Laurie Kallis

This book is dedicated to my family—to my husband Al, who has supported and encouraged me all along the way, and to my wonderful daughters, grandchildren and future grandchildren. I want them all to know where I came from and how I became the person I am today. I also want them to know how we grew up, in a life they will never know, and that we took our lot as it was dealt to us, always looking for the good and fun in life, and always living with integrity.

With love for all of my siblings, including my baby sister Filomena, twin sister of Gus, who died at six months of age.

With gratitude and love for my dear mother and, in particular, for my father, the most central influence in our lives.

Contents

My Mother

In 1998, fifty-two years after my mother's death, I journeyed back to Ottawa to attend a relative's funeral. People gathered in clusters to offer condolences, their voices falling on the plush carpet. My oldest brother, Phil, and sister, Caroline, stood in one corner of the room. A strange sensation suddenly seized me. I walked over to them and whispered, "This place gives me the creeps. I feel like I've been here before."

"You *have* been here before," they said in unison.

"This is where our mother was laid out," Phil reminded me.

"Right over there, in that room directly across from us," said Caroline, stretching her arm and pointing her finger.

My eyes followed her direction and I felt them widen as I gazed at that dreaded funeral parlour. The image of my mother lying in the grey cloth-covered coffin, in her burial dress, filled me with emotion. I tried my best to hide my rattled nerves by going on autopilot for the next hour or so.

Soon after the service, I felt compelled to walk along Booth Street so that I could peek at my first home where fourteen of us had been born, celebrations held, and our mother had died. I stood across the street from where the broken-down house once stood. I stared at the new structure of a row house and wondered what disappointments, what rites of passage, what joys had emerged from that house these past fifty-two years.

———

My mother was an naive thirty-two-year-old woman, expecting yet another baby, and vulnerable to advice from her sister and mother. She had agreed to meet with her sister-in-law in Toronto and have an abortion without my father's knowledge.

Having already lost one of her fourteen children to an unknown cause of death—a six-month-old twin named Filomena—my mother still had thirteen children to raise. She didn't have the energy to nurture any more children. She thought an abortion was the right thing to do.

"I'd rather die than have another baby," she told my then thirteen-year-old sister, Caroline, with determination.

My Mother

Using the excuse of visiting her brother for a few days, my mother travelled by train to Toronto from Ottawa and met up with the abortionist.

The bleeding began with the first thrust of the knitting needle. Soon after the abortionist completed the procedure, infection set in and poison filled my mother's body. She returned home by train in unspeakable pain and lay in her bed for two days before she started hemorrhaging. Death was inevitable. An ambulance was called.

Me and most of my brothers and sisters all lined up in the hallway outside my mother's bedroom door. I stared up at the crumbling ceiling and focused on the bare light bulb that hung from a frayed wire. We were confused as we waited.

"Why are we standing here?" asked my brother Louie. "What's happening?"

My other brother, Nunzio, age six, a year older than me, ran into the hallway. He tripped over his untied laces but caught himself before he fell, then slowed to a walk. His hand-me-down, oversized shoes flipped up and down over his heels with every step.

An ambulance attendant ushered us into the room, and waited as everyone said their goodbyes.

My mother's body trembled as she lay on the stretcher. Then she abruptly became very still. Her face was pale and ghostly, head tilted to one side, and her shoulder-length dark hair fanned the pillow in vivid contrast to her white face. I gazed at her. She managed a weak smile, but her eyes were full of shadow. She gathered whatever strength she had left and pulled me in close. Her voice so weak, it made me wonder whether I heard her or had simply read her lips, she said, "Be a good girl while I'm gone."

I nodded tearfully and asked, "What's wrong, Mommy?"

I felt gripped by a fear I did not understand.

The attendant covered my mother with a scarlet blanket that had two wide black stripes running across the bottom. The red reminded me of the blood I had seen on her bed sheets moments earlier when it was my turn to say goodbye. I had pulled back the blanket to snuggle in beside her, but the blood-soaked nightgown and mattress startled me and I stopped. My father quickly drew the covers up to her shoulders and swept me away.

My aunt, who was standing nearby, made an inarticulate sound. "Rosie," she wept. "I will take good care of the girls."

The burden seemed to weigh heavily on her shoulders.

My mother nodded and said, "The boys will do all right for themselves."

I listened in confusion as my mother spoke to my father.

"Promise me you'll keep them all together."

My father nodded his head.

"I promise, Rosie," he told her. "I'll do the best I can."

Then the harsh siren blared and the ambulance sped off into the day.

When my father returned home from the hospital the next day, we asked, "Where's Mama, Daddy?"

He knelt down on one knee and gathered us in his arms.

"Your mama didn't wake up," he said. "She's never coming home."

I pressed into my father. The older children wailed. I didn't understand what he meant. All I knew for sure was that my mommy was not coming home, and I cried.

A week before her death, my mother had been sitting on a wooden chair in the living room. I had crawled under the rungs of the chair and was looking curiously at the bulbous blue veins that branched out on her legs. Just then, the doorbell rang. Before she got up to answer it, I reached up and touched the underside of her leg, tracing the veins ever so lightly with my fingertips as if charting a roadmap.

Mamma opened the front door to a beggar asking for food.

"I can't give you anything to eat," she said, "but wait just a minute."

She crossed back into the living room to the bureau that stood flush against the wall. She lifted a doily and removed three pennies. This was her hiding place whenever she could save a little bit of money to buy new shoes for one of us.

"This is all I have," she said when she returned to the door. "You can have it."

After handing the man the money, my mother stepped over and in between several of us kids playing on the floor so that she could stir the big pot of pasta on the stovetop in the kitchen. She hummed as she dug into the pocket of her bib apron, removed a hankie, and wiped her brow.

My mother and father honoured the church and followed Roman Catholic rules with blind faith. The priest was much revered, and he visited our home regularly. When any of us were sick and could not attend mass, he made a special trip to our home and heard our confessions. He often stayed to eat with us and sometimes brought food with him to supplement the meagre meals.

Some days a sufficient food supply blessed us, and some days it did not.

Pop repeatedly went to our parish priest and emphasized the fact that he could not feed us. The priest responded by giving my father a little cash to buy food, all the while patting him on the back and telling him, "Don't be so concerned. Just make more sons for the church; it's your duty!"

Now, with the death of my mother, my father's life—and ours—changed dramatically. He seemed hazy, different in the way he walked, which was slowly, and in the way he held his head, low as if living in unfamiliar skin. His voice had a sudden quietness.

I watched him as he sat alone in the semi-darkness, huddled in a corner chair, knees drawn up to his chest like a small boy. His shoeshine kit, my brother Steve's shoes and a cardboard cut-out sat on the chair next to him. He liked to buff our shoes to a high gloss with an army-style spit and polish. He picked up the shoe brush, scraped some polish from inside the tin, and slathered the cut-out with a coat of black shoe polish. Then he slipped the cardboard inside Steve's shoe to cover the hole in the bottom.

Pop leaned back in his chair and hugged his knees again.

That day the headline in the local newspaper read, "July 1946… Thirteen Children Left To Mourn the Death of Mom."

A sea of people attended my mother's funeral. The lineup, including thirteen very sad children, stretched the length of the funeral parlour. A broken ceiling fan above us seemed a cruel joke—the humidity and the sweltering temperature on that summer day were unbearable. Perspiring people in their Sunday best, talking under their teeth in a low drone, packed the parlour. Damp hair clung to the napes of necks and light summer cottons showing dark stains clung to backs. The air was heavy and body odour lingered in the room, almost gagging me. Everyone seemed to feel the need to embrace me. I tried to pull away from the assault of hugs and kisses.

My father spoke to his friends in Italian. I sat paralyzed, listening to the familiar, rhythmic language and the wonderful music of my father's voice, so recognizable and yet so foreign to my ears. My mind floated in utter bewilderment. I sat on one of the velvet sofas that flanked the corners of the room, my feet dangling over the edge. I crossed and uncrossed my legs at the ankle, until Caroline tugged my arm and told me to "stop fidgeting." I stared into the folded hands in my lap as if they did not belong to me.

It was now time for each of us to step up, one by one, to the ruby velvet-covered double bench. A hush fell over the room. Steve knelt at the bench and lowered his head against the grey coffin. I could see that the piece of cardboard had worked its way out of the hole at the bottom of his shoe, revealing black stains on his white sock. Phil, fourteen years old, Caroline, thirteen, Steve, twelve, Gus, ten, and Josephine, nine, each had their turn at the bench.

Louie and Mike, eight and seven, and Nunzio, just six, then had their time on the velvet bench, earnestly praying with closed eyes and hands clasped so tight their fingers turned white.

Four-year-old Pat and I stepped up when it was our turn. I still had not truly accepted what had happened. It took a second to identify the woman in the coffin.

My mother had only one or two housedresses in her wardrobe, and her Sunday best was now her burial garment: a shadow-striped olive green dress with rounded neck. Two gold-tone broaches clasped the gathers just above the breast on each side. Her hair was permed and wavy, held close behind her ears with bobby pins, and her face looked pale except for slightly pink lips and heavily rouged cheeks.

What is happening to our mom? I thought. I wanted everything to be the way it used to be. I didn't understand death. She lay there in the box imprisoned, butchered and dead.

My father picked me up and held me over the coffin.

"Say goodbye to your mamma."

I did as instructed.

"Goodbye, Mamma. I love you."

I kissed her on both cheeks and stroked her face with my finger. Then my father lowered me to the floor. His army jacket scratched my skin. I noticed the sharp creases in his trousers and the shine on his boots as he lowered me.

Pop then picked up Vince, three, and Frank, two, so they could see Mama in the coffin.

And so, one by one, we said goodbye to our mother. My father lifted up baby Sam, only seven months old, and pressed the baby's tender cheek against my mother's, making kissing sounds on one side and then the other.

A long procession of mourners followed to the graveside. My father's army friends, in full uniform, stood at attention in a perfect row. The commanding officer, Captain Harrington, issued the order. "Ah–ten-shun!" Their boots clicked into place. He shouted another order to which they saluted. Sweat dripped from their damp faces as the blistering July sun beat down on their necks.

Separated

Sam

Days after my mother's funeral, Pop remained in a state of disorientation. He had to work but didn't know anyone who could take care of us. The Children's Aid Society soon took charge and placed us in foster care. The shock of our new situation and my father's absence devastated us. We had already lost our mother; being pulled from our father was almost too much to bear.

The suffering began when Children's Aid uprooted seven-month-old Sam and me from our siblings, from our support system, from communication, from our comfort zone, from what we had always known. Sam and I were placed together in a foster home. The others were separated and placed among other homes.

"When is the baby ever going to shut up?" our foster mother complained. "He never stops crying."

I watched as she brutally slapped Sam's bottom whenever he "cried for nothing." If he cried when hungry, she spanked him. If he cried when tired, she spanked him. I felt each whack to my core. When I impulsively comforted Sam by patting his head or rubbing his back, she slapped me for interfering with her discipline.

"I want my baby to stop crying," I sobbed. "You leave my baby alone," I screamed.

My foster mother dragged me away from Sam and locked me in my room, where I fell into a state of exhaustion each night listening to Sam's cries. He often vomited from force-feeding, which made me sick, too. During such feeding times, his pleading eyes always found mine. He couldn't speak, but I knew he was saying, "Don't leave me. Protect me."

I became a stronger person by standing up for my brother. Sam's mistreatment intensified my fierce loyalty to him and ultimately to all members of my family for the rest of my life.

I longed for a word of kindness and some compassion to lighten the dark times. For months, Sam and I lived in the colour grey. Our foster mother did not respect the loss of our mother. Our coming from a poor family did not render any sympathy. We needed to be treated with sensitivity and respect; instead, we lived in utter terror. Even thirteen-year-old Caroline ran away from the home in which she was placed. What would become of us?

One day my foster mother took Sam and me to the local park. Unbeknown to me, Nunzio, six years and six months old, had been placed in a home around the corner from us. We spotted each other at once and ran to hug each other, tripping and crying.

"The lady hits Sam," I cried.

I couldn't discharge the information to him fast enough. "She hits our baby, Nunzio!"

"We'll run away and take him with us," he said.

"But how?" I asked, sobbing. "Where will we go?"

My whimpers caught my foster mother's attention. I felt her piercing eyes on me.

"Grab Sam and we'll run," Nunzio said.

Once we saw the two mothers engaged in conversation, we both ran, pushing the baby carriage ahead of us, not daring to look back. The short block seemed endless. As we turned the corner, my foster mother was standing in front of us with arms folded.

During a biweekly visit with our father, I told him everything through tears. He saw Sam's serious diaper rash and flipped. His anger flared. In a violent rage, he charged to the kitchen and confronted the foster mother with a clenched fist trembling close to her face.

"If you ever even *think* of touching my children again," he screamed, "I'll break your fucking arm!"

Pop went to see the social worker the next day and demanded the return of his children. She refused to give us back unless someone was in place to look after us full time when he worked. Caroline, who was in grade eight, received special permission from the school board to remain at home and take care of us twelve kids. She cooked, cleaned, did the laundry and cared for us as best a thirteen-year-old could. She had no social life. This was her lot in life—or so she thought.

First Year of School

I don't know or perhaps I can't remember why Nunzio and I attended grade one together at St. Anthony's School; we may have been in a split class. The school stood across the street from St. Anthony's Church and a block away from our home on Booth Street. A few spiteful nuns taught us and they strapped any child who disregarded the rules.

Every morning, before the bell rang for recess, the nuns spoon-fed us cod liver oil. We lined up, awaiting our turn to swallow this awful oil, and always from the same spoon. The taste of the stuff made Nunzio vomit, and so he got into the habit of holding the liquid in his cheek, and when the bell rang, he would race outside and spit it out onto the ground.

Sister Mary Ida caught on to Nunzio's behaviour and one day tried to force him to swallow the cod liver oil before he could run outside. But Nunzio refused to comply and continued holding it in his cheek. The angry nun scrambled to her desk and removed the leather strap from the drawer. She ordered Nunzio to hold out his hand. He did. She strapped his open hand once. He grinned. She strapped his hand again. He smiled. Nunzio, now seven, simply laughed with each strike. He said the strap didn't even tickle him.

"Swallow it," Sister Mary Ida screamed.

Nunzio smiled again as the oil dribbled down his chin. She strapped his hand four times. Her anger overboiled. With each whack of the strap, her rage propelled her off the floor. Nunzio rather enjoyed torturing her with his grins and smiles. Finally exhausted, Sister Mary Ida sent him to the principal, but even he could not get Nunzio to swallow the oil. In the end, it was decided Nunzio would no longer be given the cod liver oil.

That same year I ate out of someone's raw garbage and came down with food poisoning. Pop rushed me to the Ottawa Civic Hospital and my stomach was pumped. When we returned home, Pop concocted his homemade remedy of oats sprinkled in holy water and rubbed it all over my belly. We all thought he was crazy, but his remedies seemed to work.

One day Mike, in grade two, was playing in the schoolyard on a four-foot-high cement ledge by the school fence. Another child, June Parsons, pushed him off and Mike fell and broke his arm. Children ran to him and chaos ensued. The nuns came running out with their black robes flapping and swarmed the school grounds, screaming at us to "give him space." Mike was rushed by ambulance to the hospital.

The school called Caroline, now fourteen and the caregiver of the twelve of us, to inform her of what had happened to Mike. Caroline put baby Sam in the carriage, and with the three toddlers, Frank, Vince and Pat dragging behind her, rushed off down the block to the school. She scanned the schoolyard looking for June Parsons in order to avenge the harm done to Mike. Caroline wanted to chase June Parsons down and smash in her face for hurting her Mikey.

Father Patrick came running out and stood between the two with arms outstretched to prevent them from coming to blows.

"No, no! You can't do that," he told Caroline. "Go home. Go home!"

Caroline slipped out of the schoolyard and stood by the wall with all the kids in tow and waited for June Parsons. Father Patrick noticed my sister skulking around the side of the school and scurried over to her. In an attempt to diminish Caroline's wrath, the priest led Caroline by the arm and escorted her and all the kids home. June Parsons was absent from school the following three days. She didn't appear at any recess when she did finally return and so, after some time had passed, Caroline let it go.

Mike had to wear a cast for several weeks, and we all drew pictures on it.

Not long after this incident, eight of us kids missed several days at St. Anthony's. Gus came down with scarlet fever and, of course, the infectious bacteria spread to seven others, including me. It happened near the start of the holidays and an *Ottawa Citizen* headline read, "Eight members of a family spend Christmas in the Isolation Hospital." We were put in an isolation ward for some days—and we thought it was great! We actually had clean white sheets and pillows, and three meals a day were delivered to us in our beds. It was like living in the lap of luxury.

We had fun and shared the duty of keeping watch by looking through the tiny rectangular window of the hospital room door. One of us was always on the lookout while the others jumped from bed to bed, criss-crossing and high-fiving each other. Whenever the nurse came towards our isolation room, the person on duty would yell, "Here she comes! Here she comes!" We would all collapse onto our beds, cover ourselves neatly with the blankets, and become quiet as church mice. The nurse would then insert thermometers into our mouths and find our temperatures elevated, which she didnt realize was due to all our previous activities.

First Year of School

So we were kept in the hospital longer than we needed to be. We would have loved to have extended our stay, but eventually the medication kicked in and our fevers subsided. Back home we went and then back to grade one with the crazy nuns.

What a year!

Noreen, at Marie and Al's wedding,
September 3, 1966

Enter Noreen

After my mother's premature death, we endured a few tumultuous years trying to get settled back into a regular routine.

My father took Phil and Steve, now sixteen and fourteen, to the construction site on weekends and holidays to work with him as water boys. They earned a little money, and Caroline had two fewer children to monitor.

As it sometimes happened, my father travelled on assignment with his construction crew and would stay with a local family. One such time, he was billeted in the home of Noreen Logan, or more accurately, her father's house in Hayley's Station, Ontario, a small town close to Renfrew. Noreen was an eighteen-year-old Irish Canadian. She and my father became close during the weeks he spent there, and he learned that Noreen was on the verge of running away from home, away from her strict father. Since Pop couldn't talk her out of it, he saw an opportunity. He offered to marry Noreen if she would look after his thirteen children. Her father gave his approval, and my father gave her "a way out." I'm certain she didn't understand the enormous responsibility she'd agreed to take on.

My father thus entered into a marriage of convenience with a girl who was only two years older than my oldest sibling and thirty-one years my father's junior.

The first day I met Noreen, I was impressed by her slender stature. Her skin hadn't seen much sunlight, though; it was pale and milky white. She wore a two-piece black suit with a black stovepipe hat on her head. Shiny blue-green feathers bobbed around on the hat and resembled those wiggly boppers people use at special parties.

Noreen smiled at me, and I felt a kindness of spirit.

But it was too much, too soon for Noreen to co-parent with Caroline. My oldest sister regularly locked horns with the newcomer about our upbringing. Feeling she had been replaced, and fed up with her nonexistent social life and the huge responsibilities and tasks that would have taxed any adult, Caroline ran away from home.

Noreen was not permitted to discipline us. She simply reported to Pop at the end of each day whatever antics or trouble we had gotten into and the drill would begin. We'd stand in the punitive lineup and he'd dish out strict punishment.

Pop was the classic strong-willed Italian immigrant—he alone ruled. He never really progressed in his thinking, and I often thought that he never really got "off the boat."

"Mike did this and Louie did that and Nunzio did such and such today," Noreen would report.

"No, I didn't," Louie would respond.

"Stop it! Why don't you listen to your mother?"

Pop didn't have the patience to deal with problems in a civil manner after having worked long hours every day. Immediately, his hand came down and we were punished. Not all days were like that, but many were. Noreen, in fact, didn't like to see us punished because she had a gentle heart. She tried to politely curb our misbehaviour, but she would eventually give up and shout those famous words, "Wait 'til your father gets home!"

It was too difficult for Noreen to be the affectionate, loving mother I hungered for. I still very much missed my own mother and over the years I remained quiet and withdrawn with Noreen. It was difficult for her to get close to us given the situation and my father's rules. However, the younger boys grew close to Noreen and looked to her as their mother. She was a good person, with not a mean bone in her body, and just a child herself when she wed my father. She did the best she could under the circumstances. Today I see her as a kind of Cinderella—overworked and "kept in the castle."

Noreen spent many summer days tending a garden patch willed to us by a farmer. She loved it and it seemed to relax her. She produced many wonderful vegetables and we enjoyed bumper harvests. She definitely had a green thumb.

Noreen did all the cooking and the washing.

She scrubbed the clothes in a large galvanized washtub with a scrub board. She rubbed the wet clothing with both hands and would scrub, scrub, scrub as she attempted to remove stains. Years later my older siblings, who had part-time jobs, managed to buy a wringer washer for us—a far more civilized method of washing clothes. Once the basin in the washer stopped agitating, Noreen would pick up the heavy water-soaked jeans and pass them through the hand wringer, turning the crank repeatedly.

My father and Noreen, over the next several years, had eight more children of their own, including a set of twins. However, between the delivery of all the healthy babies, Noreen also suffered three miscarriages. I was present the day Dr. Kinnear, our country doctor, appeared in the bedroom to care for Noreen. The doctor rushed to his task and my older brothers and sisters ran swiftly in a panic getting things the doctor had ordered. No one noticed me standing in the corner. I casually walked to the centre of the room, unnoticed, and stood amid the scurry and the hustle and bustle and watched. Unexpectedly, a big red blob appeared in the washbasin that Dr. Kinnear held in his hands. I gasped, horrified!

"How did she get in here?" Pop said when he heard me. "Get her out of here!"

Someone pushed me out. I didn't know Noreen was having a miscarriage and the red blob was a placenta.

Rolling Stones

The Caldwell House

Soon after marrying Noreen, Pop decided to move us to the country. He wanted us to experience open green spaces where we could run and play. He didn't want the worry of us running the streets in the city and Noreen not being able to keep track of us.

The house on Booth Street in Ottawa, with its drab interior and uneven floors, did not lend itself to joy of spirit. Although the glass in the back door did drench the kitchen with light, the bedrooms upstairs were dull, monotonous, and dark. The only colour in the living room, aside from the burgundy tufted sofa with its golden, wooden arms, was the grey that bounced from the reflection of the mirror attached to the bureau standing against the wall.

A balcony jutted out from the second floor. I recall climbing over the balcony railing one sunny day when I was about four years old. I tumbled to the ground below, screaming and hollering. It hurt so much! My mother ran out of the kitchen back door, unaware that I had flipped over the railing and fallen from the balcony above, and scooped me up.

At nighttime, the older boys kept shoes next to their pillows and threw them at the rats when they came squeaking by. A rat once climbed onto the bed where my baby brother slept next to Louie. He screamed in terror and my father came running into the room with a baseball bat that he kept beside his bed. Pop beat the rat repeatedly, right there on the bed, until the rodent split wide open. That was a scene I wouldn't soon forget. We were happy to move and be rid of the place and the rats. We were always afraid the rats would bite our faces.

In 1948, just after my seventh birthday, we gladly said goodbye and good riddance to Booth Street. We moved to an isolated area behind Uplands Airport, ten miles southwest of Ottawa. A long gravel driveway led up to a high-peaked weatherboard farmhouse that nestled between trees and vast rolling fields, where the rays of the sun cast a brilliant light across the green. A veranda encircled the entire house. I had never seen a house so large, but soon discovered that it wasn't entirely ours.

The farmhouse had been divided into two units. A man named Joe Couture and his wife occupied the other half of the house. Joe repaired cars for a living and his greasy, black fingernails were an ugly sight. His receding hairline began at the centre of his head, lending prominence to his jet black eyes. Joe's two front teeth were missing and this allowed him to perform an incredible feat—he could slip his long, pointed tongue through the gap and slither it snake-like up into his nostril and then wiggle it back and forth. We were completely riveted and all we could do was stare in awe each time he performed this tongue-into-the-nose trick. Joe loved seeing the expressions on our faces. He often sat at our kitchen table holding a cigarette in his right hand, his left elbow resting on the edge of the table with left cheek cupped in his hand. He inhaled a good portion of his cigarette with each drag. As he sucked in his cheeks, embers flew everywhere. I half-expected the cigarette to disappear right into his mouth before my eyes.

Joe's short, stubby wife always wore a dumpy housedress with stains down the front. She had rags in her hair for curlers and resembled a Raggedy Ann doll. The walls were paper-thin and we often heard their drunken arguments, which were in French. I'm sure Pop was glad we couldn't understand a word.

The schoolhouse was located in another county and therefore we could not be bussed and didn't attend school for two full years while living at the Caldwell farm.

My father thought that his children should have a dog as a companion to roam and play with, and so a border collie pup a neighbouring farmer gave us became our first pet. We named him Teddy. We found out that border collies are the hardest working of all dogs and need almost constant exercise. Teddy certainly got his due with our family.

One day, Teddy introduced us to a skunk. We ran to see what his barking and commotion was all about and saw nothing more than a black and white "kitty."

"Hold out your arms so it doesn't get away," Gus said.

We surrounded the kitty, wagon-train style. Piercing screams and yells were shouted back and forth as we hollered at each other to close the circle and catch the kitty. Teddy, of course, went crazy, and then into hunt mode, barking and growling and whining. He lowered his head, stuck his rump in the air, barked nonstop, and wagged his tail frantically.

Exhilarated, we closed the circle. Teddy backed up. We approached the kitty. The animal turned around, sprayed a putrid mist in our direction, then disappeared into the bush.

This little animal wasn't like any kitty I had ever seen.

"My eyes," Gus screamed. He spun around, rubbed his eyes, and squinted into the sun, his coveralls splattered with liquid.

"He got me, too," Nunzio yelled.

"Me, too," screamed Louie and Pat.

The "kitty" had got us all.

When we regained our senses, we gathered ourselves and faced our father. Looking at his motley crew of children lined up along the side of the house, the judge rendered his verdict.

"You stink!"

"But Pop," we said in distress, "it was only a kitty."

"It was a skunk! What did you expect to happen?"

Irritated by the stench and the number of his kids stricken, my father grabbed two of the boys and tugged them roughly back and forth as he removed their rancid shirts. He showed no gentleness during such times. Since the shirt on one son was usually saved for the next youngest in line, he was displeased even more. Pop marched down the line and made the boys drop their pants.

"Go get the shovel and dig a hole for these rags," he ordered. "And far away from the house!" he added.

Lou, Mike, Gus and Nunzio dug a large hole as Josephine, Pat, Vince, Frank, Sam and I watched. Then, Pop dumped all the clothes into the hole and herded us into the house. He opened several large tins of tomato juice—the same juice with which we made spaghetti sauce every Sunday—and poured the juice into the washtub that sat on the porch. He shoved two of us in at a time and then violently scrubbed our backs, legs and heads. The awful sensation made my stomach convulse more than once, and my nose burned from the fumes.

That wouldn't be the last time we saw a skunk, but it was the last time any of us challenged one.

On the Caldwell property, we ran free. We climbed trees, jumped off the barn roof hundreds of times into the haystack below, played hide-and-seek in the cornfield with Teddy, and played Cowboys and Indians using sticks for guns. I was basically a tomboy and ran wild on the farm with my brothers. On warm summer days, we walked down to the pond across the road and caught greasy green frogs. Although I detested snakes, I liked the feel of slick frogs slipping through my hands and releasing them from my grip, only to catch them all over again.

I had two older sisters but for several years I remained the only girl at home in a sea of boys, none of whom had much interest in playing "dolls" or "dress up." So I played rough and tumble. I was one of the boys.

There was, however, one area where my budding feminine wiles were put to good use—when it came to punishment. My father was tough but fair, a strict man who didn't appreciate being challenged by his children. He was also a smart man. With the wisdom of hard times and necessity, Pop realized that pragmatism, on occasion, was inevitable when you rode herd on a slew of kids. This meant that every now and then I caught a break because I was a girl. My gender allowed me just enough special treatment that I got away with a few more things over the years than the boys did. It wasn't much, mind you, but when you're outnumbered ten to one, you take whatever advantage you can.

I didn't have friends; my brothers filled that void. And when your friends want to run and jump and explore and climb and get dirty and smelly and bloody, well, that's what you do. Trying to back out of something with the excuse that I was a girl was met with brotherly disdain. It was altogether different if someone outside our family picked on me. But, among my brothers, I was expected to take my lumps like everyone else. My brothers busied themselves with boy activities during the long summer days, and I was happily included.

One day Nunzio found a live garter snake, bright green with a yellow stripe down its back. It had two beady eyes and a pink, forked tongue. Nunzio couldn't resist. He picked the snake up and shoved the reptile in my face.

"Gonna bite ya!" he cried with delight.

Nothing could have drained the tomboy from me faster than a two-foot-long snake. I ran to the house in a panic, crying like, well, a girl.

Nunzio tailgated me the entire way.

I ran up the stairs and onto the porch toward the front door, and then decided to change direction. Instead of running into the house and into the safety of Noreen's arms, I stayed on the porch. Clay pots with flowering geraniums sat on windowsills at about every fifteen feet or so around the encircling veranda. Nunzio chased me 'round and 'round several times. Why I didn't run inside I can't say; I was in a panic. Maybe I didn't want to slow down. Perhaps instinct told me I could be more easily cornered inside the house and I wanted to keep my options open. Regardless, I knew my brother would not stop until he had induced the maximum amount of tears and screams.

I could go on for quite a while, and so the chase continued.

Every time I looked over my shoulder, that thing was right there, wriggling in Nunzio's clammy fist.

"Stop it!" I yelled. "I hate you, I hate you, I hate you!"

For some reason, repeating the epithet quickly three times seemed to have a greater impact, like an incantation that must be uttered just so. But it didn't work because it didn't stop Nunzio!

My screams echoed across the quiet setting along with the "clomp, clomp" of Nunzio's shoes on the wooden boards as he advanced. In my mind's eye, I could see the tiny forked tongue tickling the back of my neck.

I looked over my shoulder.

The snake was right there, its head reared angrily.

The thing was probably as frightened as I was. Its little tongue lashed toward me and I jumped ahead three feet. Actually, that thing could not have been as terrified as me. I screamed louder and ran even faster, finding a speed I never knew I had. My heart pounded so hard that it sounded like thunder in my head.

"It's gonna get ya! Watch out!" Nunzio taunted, laughing even harder. "It's gonna bite you!"

Nothing could deter my brother, especially when my fear was his fuel.

"I'm gonna tell Daddy when he gets home; you're gonna get it good!"

Such threats almost never worked. Our father worked long hours and usually got home bone-tired; the last thing he wanted to hear was a trifling tale from one of us about some minor misbehaviour involving one of our siblings, and Nunzio knew it.

My screams were no longer audible. With a thumping heart and bone-dry mouth, I couldn't get a single word out. I was, officially, breathless. Terrorized, I stopped and scrambled into one of the doorways next to a window ledge, backed myself against the door, sucked in my tummy, and held both arms straight down at my sides as if this effort would make me invisible.

Clomp, clomp, clomp.

The sound of Nunzio's one-size-too-large shoes got louder and more ominous as he approached closer and closer. I picked up a potted geranium, held it above my head, and waited for him. I felt a "worzle"—that chill you get when seized with fear.

There he was!

I brought the pot down, hard.

Bull's-eye!

Blood gushed out of my brother's head like an open faucet as I watched with terrified satisfaction.

Me, 1; snake, 0. And Nunzio was down for the count.

Pop arrived home from his construction job an hour later. I ran to him first as he approached the house. The first version of a story often gets the most undivided attention, as subsequent versions tend to blur together. I snivelled and sobbed my side of the story to him about how Nunzio chased me with the snake.

"I told him to stop but he wouldn't."

Pop called Nunzio to stand in front of him.

"Have I not told you many times not to chase your sister with snakes?"

I stuck my tongue out at Nunzio from the doorway and mouthed, "Nah, nah! You're gonna get it!"

Pop took a closer look at the blood-soaked wrap on Nunzio's head and suddenly whisked him right into the car. Noreen had cleaned the wound earlier and wrapped his head in a towel to try and stop the bleeding, but it couldn't staunch the jet flow of blood. My father sped for three miles along the dirt road to Dr. Kinnear's house. The country physician patched up the wound with eight stitches.

Nunzio's injury kept him from getting a licking. Instead, Pop bought him a lollipop. What a disappointment! Where was my special treatment? I wanted Nunzio punished, not treated with candy. How dare he use an injury to get special treatment!

As soon as he got home, I got Nunzio alone and whispered, "Next time, I'll make sure you get *eighteen* stitches!" He just smiled and continued enjoying his lollipop.

After residing in the Caldwell farmhouse for two years, along with the numerous mice that gnawed away at the cardboard cartons that were our dresser drawers, and scurried and played tag throughout the bedrooms, keeping me awake on so many nights,

Pop had fallen three months behind on the rent. I saw Old Man Caldwell drive up in his Landlord Mobile. I watched him speak to Pop outside on the porch. He twirled his moustache as he told my father that we must leave.

Johnston's Corners

My father and my older brothers drove around for a few days in our old jalopy until they finally found a place to rent at Johnston's Corners, twenty miles south of Ottawa. The brick farmhouse sat at the top of a hill, surrounded by long rows of chokecherry bushes. When the chokecherries were ripe, we picked them by the bushel. Pop crushed and pitted them and made chokecherry wine.

A cemetery, located at the bottom of the gentle slope, became our playground. We played hide-and-seek every day among the tombstones. At dusk we scared each other, pretending the bodies were rising from their plots and coming to get us. It seemed all the more scary as the long summer evenings darkened. Although we never saw an actual corpse emerge from the ground, our playful screams were probably loud enough to wake the dead. Our voices outside in the darkness resonated from the bottom of the hill, especially before we were called in for the night.

One drawback to our new home, at least from a child's point of view, was that we were now close enough to attend school. At Johnston's Corners, we went to St. Mary's School, about a two-mile walk from home. The kids at the school often teased us about our lunches, which were "exotic" for the area.

"Your lunch stinks," they would say.

They didn't like the smell of scrambled eggs with green peppers. We had this lunch once a week in the fall, when peppers were plentiful. The kids were also turned off by the aroma of the meatball sandwiches in our lunches each Monday, leftovers from our traditional Sunday dinner of pasta and meatballs with watered-down tomato sauce.

One day as Pat and I were walking home from school, we passed an abundant apple orchard. The apples hung heavy on the branches, just ready for the picking. Hunger pangs enveloped us. We decided to ask the farmer's wife if we could each have an apple from their glorious, copious orchard to eat on the way home.

"Yes?" she said when we knocked on the screen door.

"Could we please have an apple to eat?" Pat asked.

She looked us up and down and then exclaimed, "There aren't any more."

Shocked, we left the porch and continued the walk home. Then Pat came up with the idea that we backtrack and pick apples anyway. We trudged back and sneaked into the orchard and, amid the hundreds of trees laden with thousands of apples, we stuffed our shirts until we could not fit another crisp, juicy apple.

We laughed all the way home, mocking, "There aren't any more. There aren't any more." How stupid is she, we cried out loud. Didn't she know that she should have said, "There *ain't* any more!" instead of "There *aren't* any more!" We hid the apples under our pillows, and that evening at bedtime, we shared them with our siblings in bed.

In rain, sleet or snow, we attended St. Mary's Church, located beside the school, every Sunday. My father, on the other hand, attended only on special occasions such as Easter or Christmas. His attendance may have been rare, but when he did accompany us to church he never failed to embarrass us. Pop always, and I mean always, fell asleep during mass. It was not unusual among some parishioners to fall asleep and it would not have been a big deal, except that Pop was a whistling chainsaw when he slept. He snored like a chainsaw, and he whistled through his nose.

Gus and Louie had to flank him in the pew and elbow him as soon as his head began to nod to jolt him from his snoring and whistling. I don't think the whistling was related to the snoring, but you never know.

Father Tompkins Visits

One winter at Johnston's Corners, temperatures dropped to twenty degrees below zero Fahrenheit and a blanket of ice covered the countryside. On one particular Sunday, the deep freeze gave us a day off from the two-mile hike to church in the merciless cold. There would be no mass and no confession that day, and for that we couldn't have been happier.

All through the previous day and night, the unstoppable force of the blizzard hammered us and it felt like we were in an arctic freeze. In the morning, the house was colder than usual, but nothing compared to the overnight wind chill with the snow, ice and howling wind. Ice and frost covered all the windows. We breathed hot air on them and wrote on the glass, just goofing around and having fun drawing pictures and writing names.

Then we learned the true meaning of the phrase "all good things must come to an end" because the joy we felt stopped abruptly when my father answered a knock on the door.

It was an ominous knock—a holy knock.

Pop opened the door and there stood old Father Tompkins, in flowing black cassock, half-frozen, looking like Frosty the Snowman, complete with hat, scarf, mittens and a pipe in his mouth. But the words he spoke were more chilling than anything Frosty had ever said.

"I've come to hear the confessions of your children, Mr. Marini. I understand many of them are down with something."

Nine of my siblings and I, infected with chicken pox, had been confined to the house for several days.

We scattered like ants on an anthill under construction. Confessing to a priest face-to-face in broad daylight was unthinkable. The confessional was bad enough, but this, today, here and now? Impossible! The very idea of Father Tompkins showing up unannounced in an ice storm—incredible! It was madness; the world had been turned upside down. Never!

"I'm feeling awful sick, Pop," Vince said at once. He was always a quick one.

"I can't confess today either, Pop." Pat followed Vince's lead. "I'm going to throw up." Frank immediately felt feverish.

Pop's eyes narrowed in anger.

Nunzio, seeing the look in my father's eyes, tried to make a run for it.

Pop grabbed him by the scruff of his shirt. "This one will be first, Father," Pop said. He reminded me of a mother cat snatching up a stray kitten and returning it to the fold.

"Pop, I don't want to go first. I don't feel so good," Nunzio whined.

"Get in there and show some respect or you'll feel even worse," Pop replied angrily, giving Nunzio's rump a kick with the side of his foot.

We all jockeyed for second, third, and fourth place, trying to get the most advantageous position. A mumbled discussion over who would say what to Father Tompkins followed; confessions about swearing, fighting, and thinking bad thoughts were always good ones. What else could we confess? We had all become familiar with the art of plotting our confessions.

Well, I won't confess in broad daylight no matter what, I thought fearlessly. There was always a moment when you didn't care what Pop said or did to you, a moment of defiance, a moment when you thought you had rights. *Confess in broad daylight?* Imagine! *Confess with my brothers in the house listening around the corner?* I wouldn't do it!

Before I knew it, I heard Pop say, "This one's next, Father." When I felt his hand on the small of my back, I felt my resolve weaken. He pushed me into the room. I was now face-to-face and eye-to-eye with Father Tompkins—in broad daylight. The sun beamed through the frosted glass, making the indoors as bright as the outdoors. This was the first time my head was not held in humility when facing a priest. With such bright light, I could see every line and every crinkle on Father Tompkins' old face, which looked kinder today and not grumpy, and for the first time I noticed the blueness of his eyes.

"What is your confession, my child?"

I knew my siblings were giggling and straining to hear me, so I glanced over my shoulder and scanned the room for prying eyes and big ears. All was clear. Succumbing to the inevitable, I heard myself say, "Bless me father, for I have sinned. It's been one week since my last confession...."

It wasn't that bad, after all.

We had lived at the house in Johnston's Corners for only a short time when we were again given notice to vacate for falling behind on the rent.

Greely

With each move we carefully packed the coal oil lamps, gently separating the glass globes from the bases and wrapping the fragile globes in newspaper.

We were getting good at it.

Our next farmhouse in Greely, Ontario, thirty miles south of Ottawa, belonged to a Mr. Desarmeau. We moved into a wreck of a house, just like the previous rentals, with no running water and no indoor toilet. Each day, we carried drinking water from the well, located about one hundred feet from the house, and lit the soaked wicks in the coal oil lamps for light at night.

Those of us who were at least nine years old worked bringing in crops for the local farmers. We were transported from farm to farm that season and billeted in different farmers' homes where we worked from sunup to sundown. A farmer would drive us home at the end of the week, and then another farmer would pick us up on Sunday evening for work on Monday morning. We handed over half of our earnings to Pop, which helped a little financially, and we were allowed to keep the other half.

In Greely, we attended a one-room schoolhouse. We were lucky enough to start school after the harvest that year, just before Halloween. It had been our first time in school during

Halloween and we had so much fun bobbing for apples and making Halloween crafts. We had never experienced this before. The teacher also handed out unsolicited treats! What a triumph! We loved that school.

School was short-lived. We didn't live in the Greely farmhouse long enough to form any attachments. After some months at the Desarmeau's farm, we defaulted on the rent. The property owner said he couldn't afford to have us stay for nothing. Again, we were faced with the unpleasant necessity of quickly finding other shelter. On no farm were we ever given a month's notice to move; we were simply given one week to clear out.

My father and older brothers drove through the back roads and on the highways again for a few days before they found another place for us to live.

Piper's

My family, now comprising two adults and fourteen children, moved into Gordon Piper's two-room house, also located in Greely. A few of my older brothers and sisters had already moved to the city to work and were sending money home to help support the rest of the family.

Inside the house, a ladder rested against a makeshift hole in the ceiling that led to the attic. We all slept up there on bare mattresses under my father's army coats and Salvation Army jackets that we used as linens. During the hot months, we gathered hundreds of milkweed pods, opened them up, scooped out the fluffy insides, and Noreen made pillows to lay our heads on at night.

A large woodstove with a reservoir sat close to the east wall in the kitchen downstairs, the only room on the first level, where we cooked our meals, ate our food, and took baths in a washtub. The roaring woodstove fire kept us cozy throughout the night and a large kettle forever steamed on top of the water reservoir at the back. A hefty crude table my father made from scrap wood took up most of the kitchen, with just enough space around for hand-made benches.

On Saturday nights, my father cleared a space under the front window and set the big galvanized washtub there for our weekly baths. No one wanted to be fourth or fifth in that tub with the dirty soap scum floating around in it.

My older sister, Josephine, turned sixteen. It was her time to leave for the big city. She moved into a rooming house with Caroline, where they shared a double bed and a hot plate. I cried when she moved away. I missed her so much because she was the only other female whom I could relate to and seek comfort from when I felt lonely. Josephine's move left me depressed—a state I fell into each time an older sibling left home—a piece of the puzzle went missing and that hole just could not be filled.

I also lost my Nonna. While living at this house, I learned of the death of my grandmother, who we sometimes travelled to Ottawa to see on Sundays.

Nonna earned her living as a bootlegger. Times were tough and people did whatever they could to survive. My grandmother was no exception. When we made the trip, all of us could not fit into the car at the same time. So we took turns. Some of us visited her one Sunday, and the rest visited her another Sunday.

We stayed at my grandmother's all day and watched people come and go out of her house with purchased bootlegged beer. She gave us lots of hugs and kisses and always held us close to her breast. My father left us with her while he played cards with a regular group at his cumpare's (one of our godfather's) house. He also sold bootlegged beer.

Nonna had arranged my mother's abortion but she accepted no blame. She insisted my father was responsible for her death, blaming his failed attempts at birth control as evidenced by my mother giving birth every year.

Bobby and Pinky

O n a hazy September day in 1951, old Naish Shields pulled his wagon into our yard and parked it under the big maple tree. "Whoa, whoa," Naish yelled, tightening the reins as the horses dodged our goose's nips at their hooves.

We ran from the field where we were playing football and greeted him with snorts and giggles. Naish climbed down from the wagon, shrugged his shoulders, and shook his head.

"Crazy kids," he muttered. "I'm here for the slaughter. Where's your father?"

————

Naish worked as a hired hand for the spinster Ruth Nevins, one mile down the road from us in Greely. My brothers Mike, twelve, and Nunzio, eleven, worked alongside Naish each day after school, tending Ruth's cattle, horses and crops. At the end of their daily work, Ruth doled out fresh milk and Maple Leaf cookies with cream filling. At home, Mike and Nunzio taunted us by smacking their lips and rubbing their tummies, boasting about these snacks the rest of us didn't have.

Although they worked with Naish on a regular basis, the boys persistently made fun of his noticeably crossed blue eyes.

"Is he looking at me, or is he looking at you when he talks?" Nunzio would ask.

"I don't know," Mike would reply. "All I know is, one 'blue' east, and one 'blue' west."

They would then drop to their knees in laughter and pound the ground with their fists. Their crack-up was contagious and sent all ten of us into fits, poking, jabbing and smacking each other. Giggling bodies soon lay scattered on the ground looking up at the sky, exhausted, arms wide open, and motionless except for the rise and fall of chests and blustery sighs.

In exchange for the boys' labour, Ruth donated two piglets and a baby goose to the family. We named the piglets Bobby and Pinky, and the goose Lucy.

We did not have a working farm, just an empty barn and a separate pigpen. Bobby and Pinky became our companions and followed us everywhere like pet dogs. Over the next ten months, they grew generously, becoming larger, fatter and taller. We kids always moved in a group and whenever they saw us strolling down the road the pigs would run from the fields and catch up with us. When we played football in the meadow, they got in the centre of everything, running when we ran, and grunting and sniffing at us as we fell to the ground.

The boys would often pen the pigs and play "rodeo." They would hop on their backs, open the pen and ride them through the fields, yelling, "Ride 'em, cowboy!"

One day Vince was riding Bobby when the pig became spooked by a rodent and started running through the field directly towards the rail fence. As Vince and Bobby approached the fence at high speed, Vince's eyes bugged out. Bobby's high-pitched squeals pierced the calm and quiet of the countryside. Unwilling to let go, Vince wrapped his arms around the pig's potbelly, held tight, and was dragged through the mud and under the rail fence. When he fell off the pig, Vince kissed the ground for ten seconds, and then stood up as the victor—one shoe off, a torn hole in the knee of his dirty coveralls, grimy hair standing on end, and chin and knee bleeding.

"I did it! I held on!" he said. "Ride 'em, cowboy!"

Laughing and pointing at him, we screamed, "You look like one of the pigs, Vince! Ha-ha!"

Bobby and Pinky and Lucy the goose wandered in and out of the house through our always-open door.

"Who the hell let these animals in the house again? Shoo-shoo, get out!" my father would yell, whacking them with the broom handle. "How many times do I have to tell you kids not to let them in the house?"

———

"I'm here for the slaughter," Naish repeated to us. "Where's your father?"

"Slaughter?" said nine-year-old Pat. "What slaughter?"

Pop had instructed us earlier that day to stay away from the barn once Naish arrived.

"We heard nothing about a slaughter," said twelve-year-old Mike.

"Where is he?" Naish asked again.

"In the barn," Mike said.

We gawked at each other in confusion as Naish walked down the slope and disappeared into the barn.

"Mr. Marini, I'm here," we heard Naish call out to our father.

We scurried after him like little ducklings after their mother, all ten of us, of different heights and sizes, from the eldest child, age fifteen, to the youngest, age six.

"What does he mean he's here for the slaughter? What slaughter?" we asked each other.

We entered the barn in silence, crept behind a stack of bales, and peered around them. We saw Bobby and Pinky standing secured to a barn post. A sledgehammer stood erect next to the pigs. Two galvanized buckets sat in the clean hay strewn on the barn floor. Naish removed his jacket, exposing a long blue-black steel dagger that hung from a leather case on his belt loop. He removed his fedora, rolled up his sleeves, swiped the back of his forearm along his forehead, and said, "Well let's get on with it, Mr. Marini."

Naish leaned over, picked up the sledgehammer, and raised it high above his head with both hands. With might and force, the sledgehammer came down hard and whacked Bobby on the head with a thud, stunning him and knocking him to the ground.

Naish briskly retrieved the dagger from the case and lunged, thrusting the blade into Bobby's throat. He missed his target and only skimmed the side of the pig's pink neck. Bobby shrieked. Blood gushed. Naish quickly and swiftly plunged the long pointed knife into the centre of Bobby's throat.

Before Naish could reclaim the knife, Bobby stood up, wobbly and still dazed, blood running from his throat like a fully opened tap. Naish tried to grab and pull the dagger out to stick it into Bobby once more. Instead, leaning too far forward in the excitement, he lost his footing and pushed the knife even further into Bobby's throat.

Bewildered and blinded by the sledgehammer wallop and the continuing assault, Bobby struggled. Squealing and shrieking, he broke loose from his tether and ran randomly about, grunting, bumping and thrashing into everything in the barn. He knocked over the galvanized buckets and ran into a wooden support beam.

Naish and my father shot forward with outstretched arms, shifting their weight from one foot to another in an attempt to corner Bobby.

The pig managed to escape between Naish's legs. He ran aimlessly from one place to another in the barnyard, squealing and shrieking, still bleeding profusely with the sharp, pointed knife stuck in his throat. He bumped into the feeding trough, staggered sideways and headed for the fence, bouncing back after he hit it. Running aimlessly, Bobby made a path straight to the barn door in a panicked, high-squealed attempt to escape but hit the wall.

"What are you doing?" we screamed. "Leave Bobby alone, Naish! You leave him alone!"

My father's jaw dropped in shock when he saw us.

Frantic, we screamed, "Let him go! Let him go!"

"You kids get out of here!" Pop hollered, pointing towards the house. His blood-spattered shirt and face added to our panic. "I told you to stay at the house. Get out. Now!"

We obediently marched up the slope, bawling and heaving quick sobs, trying not to glance back at the bloody ambush. Yet we couldn't help but look back at the slaughter and we saw that Naish and my father had finally tackled Bobby to the ground. Naish got up and whacked the pig again with the sledgehammer. This time, Bobby fell to his knees with a grunt. We ran howling into the house. In the confines of the four walls, we soon heard Pinky's squeals.

"They're hurting Pinky!" I screamed. "They're hurting Pinky!"

After a short time, all went silent.

Edging our way back down the slope, holding on to one another, we walked into the barn in a tight group with Lou in the lead. Bobby and Pinky were already strung up and slit open. The galvanized buckets swelled with the drippings of dark red blood.

A few days later Naish and Pop cut up and salted the pork formerly known as Bobby and Pinky. My father stored most of the meat in wooden barrels for preservation. He strung up some huge chunks over the beams in the kitchen to cure.

We survived 1951 with coal oil lamps, no running water, no refrigeration—and no more pet pigs.

For several weeks we barely spoke to Pop. We cast a shadow of gloom. But my father did not sympathize. On Thanksgiving Day, we sat down to a celebratory dinner. Pop and Noreen began eating. No one else touched their plates. We just stared at them, and then at each other.

"What's wrong with all of you?" my father said. "Eat! Eat! We haven't had meat like this for a long time."

Neighbouring farmers occasionally "gifted" us with meat that bordered on the questionable; meat they wouldn't eat but thought okay to donate to my family. One Sunday in church, Lou and I heard neighbours in the pew ahead of us speaking about some meat. "Give it to the Marini family. They'll eat anything," Mrs. McDonald said to Mrs. Robinson.

"I can't eat Bobby," I said.

"We can't either," said the boys. "We can't eat our pets."

We pointed at Pop.

"You killed our pets."

"Don't be so damn stupid," Pop said. "We have over three hundred pounds of perfectly good meat here. You have all worked for it. Why else did you think we raised these animals? You should know better."

"Who ever heard of Thanksgiving pork?" Lou said. "We can't eat Bobby and Pinky."

"Then you'll all go to bed without eating tonight," my father said. He always meant what he said. "Go to bed, all of you!"

Bobby and Pinky

We followed in queue and climbed the ladder to the attic, the only bedroom in the house. Blankets, strung along a clothesline, divided the room into two. One side was for all the kids, four of us to a mattress, two at the top and two at the bottom, with an assortment of throwaway coats and jackets as linen. The other side was for Noreen and my father.

Only Lucy the goose remained of the three pets, and she didn't tolerate anyone playing with her. She kept strict vigil over the vegetable patch, forbidding anyone to step into it. If you did, you would fall victim to Lucy viciously nipping at your legs and buttocks. We tried to gather the goose eggs she produced and would often run screaming into the house with Lucy in full pursuit. We ate the occasional omelette—divided by twelve, of course.

For weeks after the episode with Bobby and Pinky, we ate a steady diet of pasta with watered-down tomato sauce. Whenever Lucy allowed, we gathered a few vegetables and tossed them into the pot. My father would grumble as he attempted to introduce pork into our evening meals and saw that we always ate around it.

"We have a house with a pork ceiling," we told our friends at school. We described to them the constant reminders of Bobby and Pinky that hung from the rafters in the kitchen, visible evidence that our pet pigs no longer existed. The chunks of pork eventually turned green.

My father griped about the spoiled meat for a long time afterwards. "I just don't understand," he said. "It was perfectly good meat to eat. Forget about Bobby and Pinky."

One evening, a few weeks before Christmas, my father sat next to the glowing fire in the woodstove, deep in thought.

"What are you thinking about so hard?" Noreen asked.

"Oh, I'm just thinking about Lucy," he whispered. "I think she'll be about ready in time for Christmas dinner."

I immediately ran upstairs and told the gang.

Lucy had a stay of execution, but ended up on the dinner table anyway on New Year's Day, 1952.

None of us kids ate Lucy, either.

Not long after, the dreaded landlord's knock was sounded and we soon had to leave and find another home.

South Gloucester

This time my father found a better and brighter place, a partially furnished farmhouse in South Gloucester, twelve miles south of Ottawa. The house was situated about a half-mile down the highway from St. Mary's School and Church, saving us the two-mile trek to those institutions.

We thought we struck it rich when we saw the farmhouse. It was a vast improvement over what we had become accustomed to. It was undoubtedly the most beautiful house we had ever inhabited, and our first not slated for condemnation. This house was not at all like the other ones. There were no cracks in the plaster from which one could peek in from outside. It contained many large rooms, with walls covered in real wallpaper, and was partially furnished with a few beds. The windows let in light that flooded all the rooms.

I thought our new house was splendid. We all loved living there. We felt we had finally found not just a house but a home.

Just down the highway, about a quarter mile from the house, was a busy general store. We collected pop and milk bottles by the road and in ditches and returned them for the deposit. Then we used the money to buy real milk in small individual glass bottles, instead of drinking powdered milk mixed with water.

A Rich Poor Life

My father had told a little white lie to the owner when he rented the place—namely, that he had only five children. And so, after a week or two of living in South Gloucester, the winds of disaster swept in without warning.

The landlord had a fit when he saw more than double the number of children running around. He screamed at my father in Arabic. His face grew red and those small, round eyes of his bulged. My father screamed back. Arabs and Italians both use their hands during arguments, so the gestures flew. My father tried to explain our situation to him and pleaded with the landlord to give us a chance. Pop did his best to show him respect, but the landlord would not budge.

In a dreadful rage, the landlord pushed hard against my father's chest. "Get the hell off my property, you liar!"

Then things got really nasty. A scuffle ensued and they exchanged blows, knocking each other to the ground, then rolling around and kicking up dirt. The landlord finally broke free and ran to his truck, raving like a lunatic in his strange language. Seconds later, we heard a "clacking" sound. We turned around and saw the landlord standing about thirty feet away, holding a shotgun aimed directly at my father's head. Pop zigzagged while running at him and plowed full force into the landlord's gut, tackling him to the ground. I had always imagined him performing this technique while serving at the front in World War I.

We watched paralyzed, unable to move, our hearts galloping.

"Don't hurt Daddy!" we sobbed. "Daddy, stop!"

The two men continued scuffling around in the dirt, spitting with anger. None of us had ever seen anything like it. We were petrified.

"You get the hell off my property right now or I'll shoot you!" the landlord shouted.

Steve and Phil came out of their trance and jumped the land-lord. He somehow escaped, picked up the shotgun, and ran to his truck, shouting, "Get the hell off my property. Today!" He gunned his truck down the driveway, leaving behind a cloud of dust and fumes, the gravel slinging against the undercarriage of his vehicle. The whirling dusty blanket hung in the air for a long time, powdering the bright blue sky a wispy grey.

My father stood up, rumpled but not humbled from battle. Breathing heavily, he gathered his strength and hugged his crying children. "Okay, boys, let's get packing."

Crestfallen, I sank to the ground on my knees.

"Not another move!" someone muttered in despair.

I cried out loud. I really loved that house.

Steve and Phil returned later that afternoon in a small rented work truck with tall, wooden slatted sides. We piled our meagre possessions into the back while my father made one last inspection of the house, making certain we had taken everything. He discovered feces smeared between the sheets of one bed and urine in another.

"Steve, did you do that?"

My brother, his head down, slowly walked up to my father. When he lifted his eyes, they were clear and dry.

"Guess that shotgun scared the crap out of me, Pop."

Normally, Steve's head would have been on the block for such a stunt, even though he was eighteen years old and lived on his own. Had it not been for the unusual circumstances, Pop would have smacked him into next Friday.

My father was strict but also an ethical and honourable man. He looked at Steve for a moment, nodded, then said, "Let's go."

All our belongings stacked in the back of the truck reached well above the cab. With all us kids piled on top, Pop couldn't see out the back window. Bouncing out of the driveway, we held on for dear life, steadfast and tight, to the ropes that bound our wobbling possessions as we swayed back and forth with them.

I watched the house with a sunken heart until it disappeared behind us.

Caroline and Josephine

Marvelville

We drove around looking for a vacant farmhouse where we could either squat or rent. We spent the entire day travelling but it looked like we were going to be homeless that night. At dusk, we lay on top of our baggage, our hopes wrapped in gloom. Tired and hungry—we hadn't eaten all day—we finally found a place in Marvelville, Ontario, a tiny dot on the map, thirty-eight miles southeast of Ottawa. The abandoned house appeared sad with some windows boarded up with crossbars. There was no life around it. The grass was so tall we could barely tell where the front door might be.

Yes—we took over yet another weathered, battered, decaying house. The paint was cracked and the window frames had gone to ruin, leaving huge gaps in the wood. The steps leading up to the house were missing planks, and some of those that were there had rotted and curled up at both ends. The porch sloped to the left where someone had obviously fallen through, leaving a jagged hole in the wood flooring. The glint from the moon off the only window not boarded caught my eye. To top it all off, the ragged curtains flapping in the evening breeze gave the house a haunted look in the pale moonlight.

There were two parts to the house and one half, my father figured, could be sealed off during the winter months to save on fuel. The farmer offered cheaper rent if we kids tended his livestock daily, an arrangement Pop agreed to immediately. It was exactly what we needed—a big, unruly farmhouse for a big, unruly family.

We were finally home. We were rolling stones no more!

Marvelville Public School

Mrs. Fader

Marvelville Public School may have only been one mile from our house but by the time we crossed the south field, between the baseball diamond and the skating hut, it felt like we had hiked many more.

The one-room schoolhouse looked old with its weather-beaten but solidly built forbidding exterior. A bell hung silent and stern as we approached, oldest to youngest as was our habit. The date "1924" was engraved on the bell, the numbers somehow reminding me that we were all now three years behind in our lessons, which added to our apprehension.

The school of thirteen students had suddenly become twenty-one. Fearful and shy in new situations, my seven brothers and I lined up amid muted whispers and wide blue eyes. Some children giggled and some glared, which made us feel even more like outsiders. We were used to these reactions. Moving from place to place had taught us to adapt to new and strange situations, but it was becoming tiresome. I often wondered what people would have thought if they knew we had several more siblings who were not in school. Some of my older brothers and sisters were already out of the house and working by this time, a few attended another school, and the rest were too young for school and stayed home.

We ignored the stares as our new teacher, Mrs. Fader, patiently registered us, carefully writing our names in her ledger and looking each one of us in the eye as if silently memorizing our names. Then she suddenly rushed to the entranceway and tugged on a long, heavy rope hanging down through a hole in the ceiling. The bell came to life, sounding its iron alarm to the class and the surrounding area that school was about to start.

We filed inside and observed six rows of single and double school desks. Some of the rows comprised two grades with several kids. The other rows, reserved for one grade only, completed the ranks. I felt especially vulnerable being the only new female. I suddenly felt very much alone. Making friends had always been difficult for me; past experience and our isolated way of living left me withdrawn and silent around others.

I scanned the room and waited for further instruction.

Although the classroom was small, it appeared as vast as an open prairie. I noticed sheet music scattered across the top of an old piano in the corner of the room. A strange looking thing, which I later learned was called a metronome, rested on the centre. Large upper and lower case letters of the alphabet dominated the wall along the top of the triple chalkboards. The teacher's desk, in the middle of the room, faced the class.

Mrs. Fader

Mrs. Fader with Alice

We stood in line as Mrs. Fader had the class repeat our names while she pointed us out one by one. Some students whispered to one another in the group and rolled their eyes.

At lunchtime, I overheard Mrs. Fader tell a visitor that a friend had called her in the morning and said, "Flora, prepare yourself! There's an army of children marching toward the school."

That army, of course, was us, and Mrs. Fader was in fact prepared. She knew how to run a classroom. She presided over all eight grades by gliding up and down each row, checking work, and always encouraging us. She systematically set up the older grades by giving out reading or math assignments and then moved on to the younger grades. It was fascinating to see her in action.

"That's good work, Marie. Now you've got it, Michael. Good job, Nunzio."

Mrs. Fader turned out to be an especially compassionate teacher. She found strengths in each of us, giving us encouragement and support. But because I was so far behind in everything and showed great interest in reading, she often kept me after school for reading comprehension, and sometimes math.

I couldn't get over Mrs. Fader's rusty-red hair. I had never seen that shade of colour before. Most times she wore a kilt, depicting her Scottish heritage, and she always wore a shiny rhinestone broach at her throat, attached to a short-sleeve, see-through nylon blouse over a camisole. She dazzled me with her appearance.

We always made it to school no matter the weather conditions; we refused to stay home. Nunzio and Mike, the designated woodstove monitors, arrived at the school much earlier than anyone else in the winter mornings, often in sub-zero temperatures. They made a blazing fire in the woodstove so that when all the little kids arrived, the school would be relatively warm, and the frozen bucket of drinking water would have already melted on the stovetop. Everyone stood around the fire warming their hands or thawing their feet before class began.

During the most brutal winter months, Mrs. Fader prepared a cauldron of hot soup each icy day to help keep us all warm at lunchtime. The soup simmered on the back of the wood-fired stove all morning long and the delicious aroma made everyone hungry. She took the initiative for this, paying for the ingredients herself.

During the spring thaw each year, all roads and fields in the area flooded. We made our way to school by edging ourselves along the fence posts and hanging onto the loose barbed wire. We sprung back and forth along the wire to prevent falling into the knee-high gushing cold water. We arrived at school one day soaking wet from the wake of the quickening water, only to find the door closed and locked. We stood and shivered, staring at the locked door in disbelief. We crossed directly over the south field and through the murky flood water to Mrs. Fader's farm. We knocked on her door.

"Mrs. Fader, are you coming to school today or not?" we asked.

Astounded, Mrs. Fader looked at us and said, "What are you children doing here? The school is closed today."

We had no telephone and no hydro, so we could not know beforehand that the school was closed. We travelled home in the same manner in which we came. Our meandering forty-five minute walk turned into a two-and-a-half-hour side trip.

We got more than enough exercise by walking to and from school each day along the dirt road. If passing motorists were not courteous enough to stop and pick us up, we tailgated as they slowed down to pass us, by riding the bumper of their cars. Sometimes when the dirt roads got washed out with the spring thaw, and when the occasional city slicker got stuck in the mud, we pushed them out and earned fifty cents to share among us.

At the end of each school year, Mrs. Fader presented a brand new book to each student who had perfect attendance. We waited impatiently for that new book each June, since the only reading material at home consisted of the Saturday newspaper, comic books or *True Love* stories that Noreen liked to read. Every year, I asked Mrs. Fader to inscribe the words "perfect attendance" on my book.

Mrs. Fader inspired in us a love of reading through the stories that she read each day at 3:30 p.m., something we didn't miss for anything. Heads rested on desks, all eyes closed, and an undisturbed silence fell over the room. Then the reading began.

The imagination of each child took flight during that last half-hour of the day. I heard the amplified, rhythmic breathing of my classmate who shared a double desk with me. Every school day, I waited in anticipation for the reading, wondering what gripping adventure the next chapter of *Huck Finn* or *Peter Pan* or any other story might bring. Mrs. Fader read to the end of a chapter each day and began a new chapter the next afternoon. We always begged to hear more of the story because we didn't want her to stop. But she refused and told us to get on home.

As a preteen, I got lost in my books, but my escape into story-land at home lasted only for half an hour or so before my father would discover me missing. There was always something that needed doing on the farm. None of us could shirk our responsibilities; the ironing needed to be done, the farmer's horses needed tending, chickens needed feeding, wood needed splitting, coal needed to be carried in.

When very troubled times met us and my father could not pay the rent, I waded deeper into my books. Even in the dark of night, by the dim light of a lantern I secretly read *Anne of Green Gables* by Lucy Maude Montgomery, holding the book so close to my nose that I could barely see the words. I was afraid to cough for fear that my father might come and check on us and remove the book from my clutches. My secret thoughts and readings took me to faraway places of intrigue and wealth, away from the hopeless poverty.

In my twelfth year, I was amazed when I read a book of consequence for the first time, *Gone with the Wind*. I simply could not put it down. I read it, secretly, over several weeks. Sometimes I made note of certain passages that were unclear to me and stayed after school for private attention from Mrs. Fader. I felt as if I belonged to some special reading group consisting only of my teacher and me.

Staying late meant that I had to walk the one-mile home alone in the dark of winter on a friendless country road, without the support of my brothers. Walking home by myself scared me considerably. Each bend in the road left me feeling uncertain about what might face me at the turn of every corner. I realized that what lurked along the winding curves were merely figments of my imagination. Yet they still spooked me.

On one excursion, I reached a tree that resembled a sinister man, his long crimped arms and wobbly fingers hovering menacingly over the road, and my pace picked up three times as fast. This did not prevent me one bit from staying with Mrs. Fader until dark. I *had* to stay.

Walking home alone during daylight hours was actually enjoyable. Solitary sauntering taught me patience. I breathed in fresh air, kicked pebbles along the way, and listened to birds chirping. Sometimes I would scream out loud just to hear the echo of my voice reverberate. Often, with crushing anticipation, I would think about my older siblings coming home for the weekend.

My brothers and I longed each day to attend our one-room schoolhouse. Not one of us ever feigned sickness. School became our social club. Whenever one of us had a minor fever, several of us would get it too. All illnesses and childhood diseases spread among us like kindling in a fire. Still, we always begged Pop to allow us to go to school.

Each June when I got that new book for perfect attendance, it smelled so good—the pages crisp and untouched by anyone else. I closed my eyes and inhaled deeply as I fanned the pages close to my face. Oh, the smell of a new book gave me such a rush! I enjoyed writing my name inside the front cover, and I promptly hid my book under my mattress when I got home so that no one could touch or read it before I did. I read them over and over again.

I was told by my teacher that I had to repeat the eighth grade.

The bad news disturbed me and I cried uncontrollably. I wanted to go on with the other kids.

"Marie, your math skills are poor," Mrs. Fader said. "You children have all missed three years of schooling. Repeating the year will give you a better foundation for high school."

Settling in for another year in grade eight battered my self-esteem, but the year ahead held some promise—I still had my partial escape into Mrs. Fader's serial stories.

Mrs. Fader instilled in me a sense of self-worth. She encouraged me to learn, provided hot soup on bitterly cold days, and she believed in me.

We were the only family with perfect attendance each year and that made us all proud. I often wonder if Mrs. Fader truly understood how significant that new book was to me each year, and the great effort I made to achieve it.

The Times of Our Lives

The old car spurted and chugged and finally started. Then it stalled. It started again and spat curly clouds of noxious fumes into the air. Then it stalled again. Tensions grew as we got caught up in this drama. But our plans for a picnic and swim would not be thwarted by this deadbeat car, a 1929 Roosevelt rumble seat.

"Now we'll never get there," I said and stomped my foot. With folded arms, I went off in a huff to sulk. I loved going to the sand-pit to swim, and now this. "What a dumb car!"

Steve knelt down in front of the jalopy and inserted the crank in the portal. He wrenched it several times more. Gus sat in the front seat working the gas pedal. Sput, sput, sput.

"Yeah," we screamed and clapped and hollered. "We're going! We're going!"

It stalled again.

"Aw," we chorused in contempt.

Steve had come home for the weekend to come to the picnic with us, and now he grumbled in more disappointment than we did. He banged the steering wheel with the palm of his hand.

"Stupid car!" he shouted and climbed out. He lifted the bi-fold hood and stuck his head under it. He jiggled some wires...nothing. He kicked the thin tire. Even I knew that wouldn't help. He turned to face us and shrugged, as if to say there was nothing more he could do. But we were looking past him. He turned around to see what we were looking at, and stared at the car rolling down the embankment.

"Quick everybody, get in," he screamed.

Ten of us sprinted down the slope after the wayward car, which was quickly picking up speed. Steve, Gus and Lou raced ahead of the pack. They grabbed onto the back bumper and dug in with their heels, scraping their feet across the gravel.

"Pull back, pull back," Steve hollered as the car approached the ditch.

My father ran alongside the car and hopped into the driver's seat. "Don't hold it back," he shouted, as he turned the key. "Push!"

The car spat and chugged and the engine finally turned over just before Pop reached the ditch, then he drove in and right out again without skipping a beat. He quickly turned the car back onto the gravel and pulled to a stop.

"What are you waiting for?" he asked. "Nobody wants to go swimming?"

We happily climbed in.

The old Roosevelt shook and gasped as it idled. Made to carry four passengers, two in the front and two in the rumble seat, we managed to squeeze into every possible crevice. We arranged ourselves in two tiers: Nunzio, Mike, and Lou got the rumble seat, and Vince, Pat and I sat on their laps; my sister Jo sat between Noreen and my father in the front sat with Sam on Noreen's lap and Frankie squeezed onto Jo's lap. Jo held Frankie by the waist since she was packed in so tight and couldn't relax her arms.

Pop turned around and pointed a thick finger at Lou and said, "Hold onto your sister so she doesn't fall out." We heard this kind of order every time we went anywhere in the Roosevelt.

With a family as big as ours, this was the usual way we travelled. We loved riding in the rumble seat with the wind in our faces and our hair flying in all directions. Pop could never drive fast enough to satisfy us.

Gus stood on the passenger side running board and held on through the open window, while Steve perched on the front fender, the best seat of all. It wasn't the first time Steve held that honour.

Late one Sunday night on the way home from Ottawa after Pop's card game, Steve had to sit on the fender holding a lantern over his head to guide our way. He had to do this whenever the big round headlights burned out. We never seemed to have a ready supply to replace them. As I dozed in the backseat I could hear Steve say, "Left, Pop, now straight; a little to the right; okay, now straight. Turn left...a little to the right." Sometimes we needed both Gus and Steve to direct us home after dark, each of them straddling a fender and holding coal oil lanterns while shouting directions.

Off we went that summer day in 1952 in the black 1929 Roosevelt, speeding down the gravel road at over twenty miles an hour and looking forward to a much-needed day at the sandpit. We seldom met another car on this road, just the odd farmer pulling a load of hay with his tractor, the mailman, the milkman, or the occasional local resident or someone from a neighbouring town passing by.

The car chugged and sputtered along the unpaved road for about twenty minutes as we chatted gleefully and became more excited by the minute. At last we arrived at the sandpit and, squealing in delight, climbed out of the car much faster than we had gotten in. We were already in our bathing suits and charged straight up the steep bank of sand. Pop, Gus and Steve stayed back and unloaded. They brought everything from the car, the clanking colossal pot of pre-cooked pasta with sauce, a box of dishes and cutlery from the car's roof, the towels that dangled from the windows, and Pop's accordion that was somehow wedged up there wrapped within blankets. Then they collected wood for a fire to heat the pasta.

The sandpit stood about ten feet high with a large reservoir in the centre. Lou and Mike skimmed the shallow, muddy water, pretending to swim and splashing everyone around them.

"Stop it!" I complained. "It's cold!"

But my pleas fell on deaf ears and only made them splash me more. Nunzio and Pat followed suit.

"Pop, tell them to stop," I screamed.

"You're such a cry-baby," Mike teased, "always crying."

I splashed him back and my tears turned into laughter.

None of us knew how to swim, but not for lack of desire. We simply never had access to a swimming hole. We were having such a great time that we didn't hear Pop calling us for lunch. Steve climbed to the top of the pit and gave a two-fingered whistle.

"Spaghetti's ready!"

Famished from playing and swimming, we scrambled for the food. At the foot of the pit, Pop had spread out a blanket where he and Noreen had been enjoying a rare bit of privacy.

We ate and talked and laughed.

My sister Jo and I much preferred picnicking at the pit to picnicking at the park in Ottawa, where everyone stared at us, this large family of boisterous Italians, especially when Pop brought out the huge pot of spaghetti and placed it over the open fire. Just once I wished we could eat cold chicken and watermelon and cake and have real soft drinks on ice like the other families we'd see there. Instead, we lugged huge pots and drank water from the water fountain—if you could get near it without being squirted by my brothers. To them, water fountains were just another toy.

But our embarrassment of pasta in the park paled in comparison to my father pulling out his accordion after lunch.

"Oh, no," we'd groan, with rolling eyes and hanging heads. "We don't want to sing."

But Pop always pulled out his accordion anyway.

"Get over here and sing," he'd order. "All of you!"

We'd drag ourselves up to the fire and sit in a circle.

Stimulated by the accordion's hum of one of our favourites, "Lazy Mary," we sang, "Lazy Mary will you get up? She answered back, I am not able." We drew inspiration from one other and sang boldly as intense stares burned our backs.

At that time, Pop worked for the Department of Highways and on some weekends he brought home the big truck that carried ten of his crew and all their equipment, and we all got to go to the campsite where he worked with his crew during the week. We would stay overnight in a huge army tent that had been erected at the site. Inside were rows of cots ready for the men on Monday morning. A black cook stove stood at the centre of the tent with a stovepipe sprouting through the roof.

Glorious weekends were spent there. We'd play with crazy abandon through the surrounding fields far away from the prying eyes and stares of the park in Ottawa. The only encounters were with occasional cows lazily chewing their cud. On some Sunday mornings at the campsite, we'd stand around the cook stove watching Pop flip flapjacks into the air with a pan in each hand.

"Whoops, here it goes," he'd say, flipping them with real flair.

"Whoops, there it goes," we chanted in unison, watching the flapjacks barely miss the canvas roof of the tent before falling back into Pop's pans. Noreen, in charge of the corn syrup, poured the syrup onto the flapjacks as we stood in line.

Unlike at the Ottawa park, we didn't mind singing at the sandpit. In fact, without onlookers, we truly enjoyed it. By the end of the day, we were all worn out. When we headed home at dusk, again all seated in our familiar layered tiers, we fell asleep on each other like newborn puppies, happy and exhausted from the day's activities.

Life was simple at both the sandpit and the campsite. Pop took us to both places whenever he could. It never got better than that. We didn't have much, but we did often have fun. Those were the times of our lives.

Sam, Teddy and Frank

Travels with Teddy

The only pet we ever had was Teddy, a typically rambunctious border collie that we acquired at the Caldwell House. Our father tolerated more than loved him, but for us kids Teddy was a wonderful companion for many years.

Teddy was like another sibling, except without all the arguments and complications. He never teased nor told on anyone. He was always in a good mood, never grouchy, whiny or sad—the perfect playmate for a large group of children always engaged in one conflict or another. Teddy was a pet in whom any one of us could find solace and comfort no matter what. He was always there, ready to run or play, or just look up at us with those big brown puppy-dog eyes and make everything a little better. It was impossible to be sad when Teddy was around. He became an important part of our lives. Whenever he was needed, Teddy was right there.

"A dog's place is outside," my father would say for the umpteenth time. "That's where he belongs."

Locked out at night, Teddy would bark on and off under our bedroom window all night long. You can imagine the heartbreak we all felt listening to our best friend tell us, in the only way he could, that it was cold outside!

We felt Pop's heart was colder.

When I look back now, I marvel at how my father was able to handle so many kids, let alone a playful pup. I'm surprised a few of us weren't out there with Teddy.

But of course we weren't going to let sleeping dogs lie, or a barking one lie outside in the cold.

The solution eluded us for a time until someone came up with the answer—a ladder. The idea was brilliant. All we had to do was teach Teddy how to climb a ladder to our window. That turned out to be the easy part. It's amazing how quickly a dog or person can learn something like that when the temperature outside is below freezing. The difficult part was setting up and taking down the ladder. We couldn't very well leave it leaning against the house for my father to see.

We hid the ladder behind a clump of pine trees below the window. After Pop was asleep, one of my brothers would hang out of the window while four others held his ankles. Ever so carefully, he pulled the ladder into place, afraid that if the ladder scraped the side of the house or fell, it would wake up my father. Pop was a pretty sound sleeper but he was also a parent. Kids know that a parent's hearing is specifically tuned to the frequency of their children's activities, especially when it comes to danger or shenanigans; this probably qualified as both.

Once he was proficient at climbing the ladder, Teddy began to enjoy it. To him, it became a game. His bark was our signal. With the ladder in place, Teddy was coaxed up one rung at a time.

"Come on, Teddy! Good boy, Teddy! Come on!"

It was quite an operation and I imagine it would have been a strange thing to see from outside of the house, but Teddy's woeful eyes, flattened ears and laboured breath were a sight to behold from above. Often the rungs were wet or icy, and there were quite a few close calls, but we always got him up. When he reached the top, we pulled Teddy in.

During Pop's nightly "barracks check," we hid Teddy under the covers or on the floor between the bed and the wall. Things worked beautifully for a while, but my father was no fool. It's awfully hard for children not to smile when they're getting away with something. Pop must have seen something on one of our much-too-innocent faces because one night after bed check, he waited out in the hall for a moment, then quickly opened the door and saw Teddy warming my brother's feet at the end of the bed. This was Teddy's primary duty in exchange for lodging; he was passed back and forth like an extra blanket.

As soon as he saw Pop in the open door, Teddy knew he was in trouble. He leapt off the bed and scooted out the door with his tail between his legs. Satisfied that the interloper had been evicted, Pop went back to bed, never stopping to wonder how we'd been able to get the dog past him. Since he did not ask how we managed to sneak Teddy inside, we naturally continued our unlawful ways and simply waited a little longer before breaking out our four-legged heater.

The old farmhouse didn't have insulation and when the winter winds came howling through the pines from the north, and ultimately through the cracks in our walls, Teddy was the subject of nightly arguments. Every one of us wanted to sleep next to him to keep warm.

"It's my turn," I would say.

"No, it's *my* turn," Pat would say.

Since the room held three double beds with four kids in each one, we finally settled on a rotational method of sharing Teddy.

Two female dogs, one a German Shepherd and the other with a bit of wolf in her, appeared on the farm the following winter. Pop constantly shooed them away, but they were obvious strays and seemed to have nowhere else to go. Despite my father not letting us feed them, the dogs managed to survive on whatever they could find in the wild and usually stayed around our farm.

With the spring thaw, the creeks ran high and swift. One rainy day, Queenie and Banjo, as we had named them, each gave birth to nine pups in our barn. Overnight, our canine population increased from three to twenty-one. The equation was simple to us: each kid could have their own dog!

Our Teddy, the proud papa, doted on the pups and groomed them as much as their mothers did. Whenever one of them strayed from the group, he would pick it up by the scruff of its neck with his teeth and deposit it back into the fold. It was adorable.

But it didn't last.

After a short while, Pop gathered us for an announcement. In his typical, unsentimental way, and with a furrowed brow, he gave us the bad news. "We can't feed all these pups," he said. "They have to be drowned."

We stared back at him in shock. After a brief moment of silence, the floodgates opened. Oh, did we cry and beg.

"Pop, no! We can share our food with them! Please don't kill them, Pop!"

But our father, as always, was firm in his decision, and he ordered Lou, Mike and Nunzio to dig a grave.

"Three feet long, one and one half foot wide, and three feet deep," he told them.

Pop was a demolition expert and a whiz at math. He knew his dimensions.

"Gus, you find a heavy rock. Pat, you get a potato sack from the barn, and the rest of you gather the pups."

Defeated, we went about our tasks. We knew better than to argue.

"Gus, put the rock in the sack to anchor it. The rest of you gather the pups and put them in the sack."

We did as we were told. The pups were still suckling, which made us cry even harder. As we knelt down and pulled them away from their mothers and placed them in the sack, the pups ran back out and scattered. We had to chase them down and return them to the sack. I couldn't help but notice our actions resembled Teddy's—picking up the errant pups and putting them back in the fold with the rest.

When all the pups were finally in the sack, Gus stood up and twisted the top, taking his time, and Lou knelt and tied it with binder twine. It took a long time to finish this heavy task.

"Gus, take the sack down to the creek and throw it in," Pop ordered.

"Why do *I* have to drown them?" Gus cried.

"Do as I tell you!"

Gus put the sack over his shoulder and walked unsteadily toward the creek. Lou, Nunzio and Mike cried as they stayed behind and dug the grave.

The rest of us followed Gus across the field, his slow and solemn pace making for an appropriate funeral procession. We cried our way down the hill and over to the bank of the swift-running creek. Arriving at the bank, we stood there staring at the water and briefly considered an insurrection. Pop seemed to sense a mutiny brewing. His scowling face and puckered brow betrayed his own uneasiness. I think he hoped that Gus would just toss in the sack of pups without being told again, but that was obviously not going to happen.

Pop paced back and forth and finally said, "Just do it! Throw them in—now!"

At that moment, Teddy came running up and sniffed the sack, whining and searching in vain for his offspring, with Queenie and Banjo underfoot. They circled the sack and barked persistently. Pop angrily ordered that they be locked up in the barn for the night.

Crouching at the bank, Gus dipped his hand into the icy water. It was getting dark and the water had suddenly turned much colder and blacker, as if the creek itself was saddened by what was about to unfold.

"Gus," said Pop, his voice low and menacing.

My brother then swung the sack and threw it toward the dark water. The bag landed with a sickening thud in the shallow water smack in the middle of the creek. We stood in stunned silence. No more pups yelping. No more mother dogs barking. No more Teddy whining. No more kids crying. It was as if all the life had gone out of us as well.

After several minutes, Pop ordered Gus to retrieve the sack. He waded into the cold water, found the limp sack, and carried it up onto the bank. His eyes looked haunted. Once more, Gus led the sad parade up the bank and through the field to the back of the barn where Lou, Nunzio and Mike stood at the edge of the open grave. It had been dug to Pop's precise dimensions.

Two of the boys gently lowered the weighted-down sack into the hole. This triggered another round of tears to end the arduous, unforgettable day. The boys picked up their shovels, struck the dirt and filled the pit, one shovelful of dirt after another until the hole was covered.

"Alright," Pop said. "Up to the house for supper, and then bedtime."

Gus stomped and cried all the way into the house, followed by the rest of us as we sadly muttered to each other. Gus refused to eat, claiming to have no appetite. Sam, Frank, Vince, Pat, Nunzio, Mike, Lou and Josephine also declined dinner and followed Gus up the stairs to bed. Fully charged by the day's drama and devastation, we eventually succumbed to sleep at some point during the night. I think we must have cried ourselves to sleep, knowing we would never see those pups again.

Just as an orange ribbon appeared on the horizon, we awoke to the sound of crying. But the cries we heard weren't human. It sounded like...the pups! We jumped out of bed and pushed and shoved our way down the stairs and outside. Had it all been some terrible dream?

It was daybreak and it took a moment before our eyes adjusted to the incredible sight. And what a sight it was! Queenie and Banjo were lounging against the back of the house and the pups were vigorously feeding, emitting little grunts and cries of hunger and satisfaction. Next to them, Teddy kept watch and went back and forth between the two mothers, grooming the pups as they suckled.

At some point during the night Queenie and Banjo, locked in the barn, had dug under the barn door from the inside, while

Teddy dug from the outside through stones and hard dirt, releasing the mothers to their resurrected pups who had somehow survived their drowning. Bloody paws and torn nails revealed the powerful measures they had taken as we slept. Not only had they dug their escape from the barn, they had also dug down three feet to the sack and had torn the burlap to shreds. They had released their babies!

None of us said a word. We watched, astonished, our mouths agape, as the pups fed. It was as if the combined weight of our collective prayers had compelled the Lord Himself to perform a miracle on our farm during the night. There were simply no words adequate for the occasion.

Pop was a religious man. When he walked out of the house barefoot and sleepy-eyed, we could tell from the look on his face that he, too, had seen the light. He felt the events of the night had signified divine intervention. If the good Lord wanted these pups spared, he would do nothing further to interfere. He also didn't have the heart to do away with them again. But that didn't mean he was suddenly able to feed his children and twenty-one dogs. For the next several weeks, any visitor from the city left our farm with a puppy. Eventually they were all given away and the two mothers moved on.

We enjoyed Teddy for another thirteen years. His fifteenth year brought failing eyesight, a lack of appetite, arthritis and only God knows what else. As he did many years before, Pop gathered us again. His direct words hit home hard.

"Teddy has to be put down."

Pop explained that Teddy was sick and suffering, and though we protested, we all knew he was right. I've always thought that our father saw a little of himself in Teddy, something he would have probably laughed off as sentimental hogwash. After all,

Teddy was only a dog. But even though Pop was still a strong man at that time, the years had also taken a toll on him. Like Teddy, Pop would have done anything to protect his children, and after the drowning fiasco, I believe I saw a kind of kinship between Pop and Teddy, as if they each sensed the other's devotion to family.

My brother-in-law John agreed to do the deed.

Teddy's final minute arrived. After the summer of the skunk, the winters of warm feet, the play-fighting, and the miracle at the creek, as well as hundreds of other adventures, it was time to say goodbye. We watched John lead Teddy, who didn't know his fate, into the bush. It was so quiet I could hear my own heartbeat. And then we heard the shot of the rifle. It sounded like a branch snapping, and I naturally looked to the forest expecting to see a tree teetering and falling against the light blue sky. But everything was still.

Then we heard a cry, a full-throated yelp.

I'll never forget that moment or that sound as long as I live. It was as if I'd been hit by a bolt of lightning. The shot resounded and reverberated across the terrain. We tracked to the bush with shovels in hand and took turns digging a grave for Teddy. We made a cross of gathered twigs, tied them together with binder twine, and said a prayer for our long-time best friend.

Confirmation

H ere I come," Pop said as he rushed across the kitchen floor with a gigantic dented pot in his hands. I stood around the twelve-foot long rectangular table with eight of my brothers, each of us at our "stations," and eagerly watched my father dump twenty pounds of mashed potatoes onto the centre of the table.

On special occasions like confirmations, baptisms and religious holidays, homemade gnocchi was the order of the day. Whenever a confirmation rolled around, those closest in age were confirmed in small groups. On this day, two of my brothers and I were to be confirmed, so a celebration of family and friends was to ensue with singing and dancing and eating everything in sight.

Feverish preparations had taken place hours earlier. We peeled the potatoes, boiled them, and let them cool. Following a second scrubbing of the porous table surface, we used toothpicks and matchsticks and picked out residual specks left in crevices that the scrub brushes couldn't reach. We looked forward to the joy of working in the mixture of flour, mashed potatoes and eggs. Pop bordered the lumpy potatoes with a ridge of flour. Closing his fingers, he swirled his hand 'round and 'round, creating a deep hole in the centre of the heap. Cracking eggs one at a time with one hand, he separated the yolk from the whites and tossed the yokes into the hole. We counted in pitched voices as yolk after yolk sailed into the volcano of potatoes.

"That's one! That's two! That's three!" we cheered and clapped until all the eggs had been counted.

Pop added a bit of oil to the mixture and swept the flour back and forth, thrusting the heels of his hands into the great load of dough, the table creaking in rhythm to his every move. Then he broke into song.

"When the moon hits your eye like a big pizza pie, that's amore!" He stopped and shouted cheerfully, "Come on, sing! Sing!"

We sang. "When the world seems to shine like you've had too much wine, that's amore!"

As he doled out rounds of dough to each of us at our stations around the table, we worked the way we had been taught many times before. The dough felt smooth and warm under my fingers. I pushed it back and forth with the heel of my hand and fingertips, keeping rhythm with Pop and the creak of that old table. I always believed that making gnocchi was designed to teach us the art of pitching in because it always lifted our spirits. This day had been no exception.

"Keep going, kids. I'ma get some more flour."

Now I can't speak to the folly of leaving children in a room with that much dough, but in our family, let's just say Pop was asking for trouble.

Frankie sang, "When the moon hits your eye..." Then, to much laughter, he pulled a wad of dough from his chunk and slung it at me from across the table, hitting me square in the eye.

"I'm gonna get you for that, Frankie!"

I picked up the dough and threw it back at him, hitting him smack in the forehead. Now I was laughing as hard as the others.

Pat pulled a chunk from his round of dough and heaved it at Vince. Nunzio yanked a piece and threw it at Mike. Gus threw one at Sam. Control walked out the door and in stepped anarchy.

Pop came running in with the sack of flour, shouting, "What the hell are you kids doing? Stop it before you all get a good boot!" He illustrated his point by cracking a couple of nearby heads. With so many children about, there were always nearby heads. "Now get back to work!"

Pop left the room again to wash the big pot—mistake number two!

Nunzio, never one to miss an opportunity, rolled a piece of dough into the shape of a snake and hurled it at me. I squealed and everyone else howled in delight. Pop reappeared and a hush fell over the room. He glowered. Then, he sighed. I think he knew he was going to crack a lot of heads that day.

That night, as he ordered us all to bed, Pop said, "Tomorrow is a big day. Get some sleep! After the ceremony, we hava biga party!"

We scurried off to bed, anticipating having a great time and plenty to eat the next day. I think Pop was just as excited as we were. At some point during the night, I had to use the bathroom. I shook Pat.

"Come to the outhouse with me and hold the lantern."

"Get someone else," he said and rolled over to go back to sleep.

"I always go with you," I said. "Please...you have to. Come on."

"Too tired," he whined. But then he wiped the sleep from his eyes and swung his legs onto the floor. "I don't wanna be out there all night, so you better hurry."

At night, we used the buddy system to visit the outhouse because it could get pretty eerie out there in the pitch-dark countryside. Pat followed me through his sleepy haze to the out-house. We tiptoed down the stairs and into the night, walking down the black path and swiping past protruding branches. The wind picked up and the trees whistled. The crisp night air and the distant howl of wolves sent a chill right through me. I shivered. We ran down the path, the handle of the dim lantern rasping back and forth in Pat's hand.

"Hold the lantern up, Pat. It's hard to see."

At night, I had to reacquaint myself with the path. We passed the stunted bushes. Scared of the shadows cast by the lantern, we edged our way and stuck close together. Teddy followed us. We weren't aware that Frankie was sneaking down the path in the pitch black behind us.

Pat stood outside the outhouse shivering in his pyjamas, while I sat on one of the holes on the two-seater. Sometimes my sister Jo and I would go together and we'd flick through an old Eaton's catalogue and talk about what we would buy if we had money. Then we'd tear out a page and use it for toilet paper. The pages with items we liked were saved to wipe last. I'd just sat down when I heard a branch snap.

"What's that?" I asked, and held my breath. "Did you hear something, Pat?"

"No," he said. "Just hurry up. It's cold out here!"

I relaxed on the seat.

I felt a switch brush against my backside and saw that it came through one of the cracks in the outhouse wall.

"Snake!" Frankie screamed.

I screamed. Then Pat screamed. And Teddy barked.

I jumped up and shoved the door open, knocking Pat flat on his back. I ran screaming, pulling up my pyjama bottoms as I struggled up the hill with Pat close behind me. Our screeches shattered the night. Teddy barked continuously. Tugging and pulling at each other's sleeves and bumping against each other all the way, we were like two mad roller derby champions—both of us wanted to be the first one up the path.

The lantern in the window was our beacon in the pitch-black night. We ran towards it. Frankie brought up the rear, laughing his fool head off. Pop's frame suddenly filled the doorway, his arms crossed over his chest, one foot drumming the floor. He huffed and puffed like a mad bull about to charge. There was nothing we could do but face his anger head on. We ducked through the doorway, tripping and falling over each other, as Pop knuckled us over the head and booted each of our behinds.

"You're gonna wake the dead! Get to bed and if I hear another peep out of you, you'll be joinin' 'em!"

In the morning, Pop lined us up and said, "If I have to speak to any one of you today at the party, you gonna be sorry."

None of us wanted that.

As it turned out, the party whirled without a hitch and everyone had a great time. In the late afternoon, I changed out of my confirmation dress to go outside and play. Pop had to pry the pink nylon dress with the tiny floral pattern from my clutches. I wanted to keep the dress.

"Give it to me, Dolly," he said. "I have to give it back to your aunt."

Tears ran down my cheeks and onto the dress as I gave it up. Pop took me into his strong arms and whispered in my ear, "You couldn't wear it any place else, you know. One day you'll own a nice dress like this one."

I nodded and wiped my face on his shirt. He cupped my face in his rough hands.

"Go play now. Go on."

Once outside I scurried to the bank of the creek and slid down the muddy slope to listen to the rippling of the water from the spring thaw. I kneeled at the creek's edge and scooped up the cool clear water, hearing neither Nunzio nor Mike behind me nor seeing their reflection in the water. They were preparing to scare me again.

Just another day on the farm.

Caroline

Pop's Accordion

E ach time my father announced, "Get ready for bed, and then we'll sing," my siblings and I scurried like demented little mice. Gus, Vince, Lou and Pat, who were self-taught musicians, would pick up their beat-up guitars. Pop would strap on his old accordion that he had bought shortly after immigrating to Canada in 1916, and as always, move the weathered pleats in and out, holding his ear to the keys as he tested for just the right sound.

When they were all tuned up and ready to go, we would link arms and belt out one of our father's favourites, "That's Amore."

"When the moon hits your eye like a big pizza pie, that's amore!" We swayed back and forth and sang with all our might. "When the world seems to shine like you've had too much wine, that's amore!"

We loved singing together and the farmhouse was our favourite place because it seemed to lift our voices. Perhaps it was the acoustics in the big old place, or the fact that there was no one to hear us for miles.

One night, some of us noticed how carefully Pop had returned his accordion to its case. His instrument had been looking fragile of late. We decided to band together and buy our father a new accordion. Caroline collected hard-earned money from my older brothers, Phil and Steve, the result of their toil and sweat at menial jobs. She also chipped in what she had saved for an emergency. Phil and Steve accompanied Caroline to Little Italy in Ottawa and bought Pop a brand new accordion—well, new in the sense that he had never played this particular accordion before.

We set out to surprise Pop on his birthday the following Saturday. Filled with excitement at the idea of pulling one over on our father, we eagerly awaited the arrival of Caroline, Phil and Steve, constantly running back and forth to the window. Finally, late in the afternoon, Pat, Sam and Frank screamed, "They're here! They're here!" when the three intrepid treasure hunters pulled into the driveway with the precious cargo.

Frank and Pat managed to pull Pop away from stirring the pasta sauce on the woodstove so that he wouldn't be able to see the accordion being brought into the house. They escorted him out the front door with the excuse that he needed to examine the porch boards that had rotted away.

While Caroline, Phil, Steve and Gus came into the house through the back door, our father surveyed the porch damage. Pop must have found this strange since the boys had been assigned the repair job. I believe Pop at this point may have suspected something was up. It was, after all, his birthday. But as any parent soon knows, half the fun of such surprises is the look on the faces of the children. If he knew anything, he didn't let on.

"It's time!" Caroline called out. "Everyone come into the living room. Hurry!"

Frank and Pat yanked Pop into the house by the arm and we all yelled in unison, "Surprise!"

"Happy birthday, Pop," Caroline said. "We all chipped in and bought this brand new accordion for you."

His eyes widened, his chest swelled, and his cheeks were wet when he rushed over to his gift.

"Where did you get the money?" he asked. "How did you do this?"

I knew then that Pop hadn't had a clue. Speechless, he threw his arms open and every one of us ran into the huddle. Kids piled on top of each other to get in on the action as Pop fingered the keys on his new accordion, tenderly stroking its features as if it were a sleeping cat. He pulled it out, quickly found a key, and began tapping his foot. The boys hurried for their guitars to catch the rhythm. Pop fanned out the accordion wide and began to sing.

"Lazy Mary will you get up, she answered back I am not able. Lazy Mary will you get up, we need the sheets for the table!"

He knew we loved that song!

The quick pace of "Lazy Mary" got us on our feet. We pushed the chairs against the wall and linked arms and swung each other back and forth, our feet leaving the floor on each turn. We danced, we laughed, we sang, until we were completely exhausted.

Pop loved his new accordion and he loved gathering us to sing when we had company. We were the featured act for all visitors who graced our home. Without a thought, our group sang for people on demand at our house parties. During celebrations like baptisms and birthdays, our guests sang and danced right along with us.

After a while Pop finally closed the accordion and announced, "Okay, time for bed."

We all moaned.

"Church in the morning," he added.

Still excited, we bombarded Pop with requests for special dispensation.

"Aw, just when we're having fun."

"Can we stay up just a little longer?"

"Please, Pop?"

"I don't want to tell you a second time," he said.

We all knew it wasn't prudent to argue with him. He always meant what he said. With Pop, rules were rules. We always knew where we stood with him.

On the other hand, challenging Pop was also an inevitable rite of passage. This momentous event in the lives of his children occurred around the age of sixteen and was a very big deal to the challenger. But as a man who'd raised twenty-one children, Pop had simply heard every defiant variation and could counter them all. He was steadfast and unwavering. He was the undisputed champion. We younger ones had witnessed our older siblings being turned out to fend for themselves—to work and send money home.

The night before he turned sixteen, Gus had come home after curfew. An argument ensued. Pop refused to bend the rules even for a sixteenth birthday. His children listened to him—or else.

It was Gus's turn to challenge Pop's authority, just as all his elder siblings before him had. "I'm old enough to stay out late!" Gus whined. "I'm sixteen now!"

Pop whacked him on the side of the head.

"If you can't follow my rules, then go out there in the world and find your own way!"

Gus had left that same night, hitchhiking to Ottawa, thirty-eight miles away.

I had cried and begged for him to stay before he left. "Don't go, Gus! I don't want you to go." Every time one of my siblings left home, they took a piece of my heart with them.

"Don't worry," he had answered. "When I find a job and get settled, I'll come back to visit."

In spite of our father's strictness we all felt obliged, without question, to honour him; it was unthinkable for anyone to leave home and not ever return.

Gus coming home with Caroline and the boys for Pop's birthday celebration was his first visit home. Gus's argument with Pop was still fresh in everyone's mind. So at the sound of the words, "I don't want to tell you a second time," the boys picked up their instruments and placed them under the paint-chipped windowsill.

A lineup formed with Lou at the front. He reached up and kissed Pop's cheek. "Goodnight, Pop."

"Goodnight, son," he said.

Next was Pat, followed by me, then Frank, Vince, Mike, Sam, Tony, Nunzio and Josephine.

And finally, Gus.

As Pop hugged him, he held on longer and whispered, "Glad you're home, son."

Anger never lasted long in our house. Reconciliation came with the first visit home.

Pop's Accordion

When the following Saturday rolled around, the noise level reached new heights. Chairs grated along the bare floor as the din of energized children prepared to vie for their position in the familiar circle. Pop carried his new accordion in one hand, dragged his chair along the floor with the other, then sat down like a concert pianist on a world stage. He opened the case and gently blew across the keys, lightly dispersing the week's dust. He propped the accordion on his knee, placed his left hand under the thick leather strap, and toyed with the buttons. The red frame of the accordion gleamed in the radiance of the fire. Pop placed his right fingers on the keyboard and gave a nod of his head.

We sang and swayed to the music, the flames of the fire from the potbelly stove dancing right along with us. The look on Pop's face was priceless. He never looked happier than when he watched his children sing.

Trick or Treat

In the pitch-black night, we headed toward a lonely beacon shining at the top of a barn. Trick or treating on a mostly desolate country road was scary business, taking fifteen minutes just to walk from one farm to the next, only to be handed one lousy apple per neighbour.

"It's easier and quicker just to steal the damn apples from them," Mike said.

True, but then we would not have got to experience the Halloween ritual of trick or treating.

The group ran on ahead of me to the farmhouse. What happened next is a hazy memory. I screamed, "Wait for me! Don't leave me! I'm scared," and ran breathless to keep pace with my brothers. I heard a rustle in the ditch. My heart quickened. I ran faster. The rustling came closer. I yelled for Pat and cried at the same time, barely seeing the path in front of me.

Tiny lights shone in the ditch and were coming my way fast. Instinct told me it was the eyes of a glaring animal, possibly wolves from the bush. A tree that I hated passing after dark, which resembled a scary man with outstretched arms, came up on my left. I heard the boys' voices in the distance and screamed for them again.

"Come back! Wait for me!"

I dropped the potato sack that held my apples and sprinted up the road with the finger of fear pressing into the small of my back.

Halloween at Marvelville was not fun. The uneven and pot-holed terrain mixed in with the too-black night was almost unbearable. On the other hand, I enjoyed the indoor Halloween day activities arranged by the Greely school teacher. Bobbing for apples, holding the candies that she handed out and making paper jack-o'-lanterns was better than any Halloween trick or treating I ever experienced.

Nunzio

The Runaway Tractor

At dusk on a chilly evening in early May of 1952, the bright lights of a tractor appeared at the end of our long, narrow driveway. My father and all us kids ran to the window and looked out. Visitors excited us because we rarely had any, and they eased the isolation we often felt on the farm. Next to my father's accordion playing every other Saturday night, nothing grabbed our attention as much as the occasional visitor did with news and stories from the outside world.

The lights of the tractor and a car that followed bounced up and down as they made their way across the deep ruts in the driveway caused by daytime thaws and nighttime freezes. Everyone scrambled to answer the knock at the door. A gusting wind blew the doorknob out of my hand as I opened it and snowflakes wafted in.

"Good evening, Mr. Desarmeau," Pop said. "What can I do for you?"

"Mr. Marini, I just wanted to let you know that I'll be tilling the east field in a few weeks and I've come to leave my tractor here," he replied. "Could you keep an eye on it for me?"

"And be sure nobody touches it!" said his snobby son, looking at me and my brothers.

Lou had beaten up the obnoxious little creep a month earlier, giving him a bloody nose for calling us "dirty Wops." Since then, he only came near us when accompanied by his father.

We rented this decrepit farmhouse from Mr. Desarmeau, and cared and fed his livestock in exchange for dirt-cheap rent. Little had we known that it also came with putting up with his obnoxious son. On occasion, when we could not afford to buy powdered milk, we partially milked three or four of his cows before he and his son arrived to do their daily milking. I'm sure Mr. Desarmeau suspected us, but never accused us because he couldn't prove it.

We woke up the next morning to the clack of the metal toaster doors flipping open and closed against the planks of the kitchen table. My father arose daily at five in the morning and kept a close watch on the bread toasting two at a time. After one side was toasted, he opened the two metal doors of the toaster, flipped the bread over, and continued toasting the other side until one hundred slices of bread had been toasted. Pop threw a handful of coffee grounds into a pot of boiling water on the stove and the aroma, along with porridge cooking in the cauldron and the smell of wood burning, always brought us downstairs.

Once the outside chores had been completed—the animals fed and watered, troughs cleaned, and wood chopped for the next day—we were free to run and play until called in for supper. We passed the days playing baseball, walking the high beams in the barn and jumping from the loft window into the haystack below. "Bombs away!" was the cry as the boys jumped onto the haystack and then rolled to the ground and headed back into the barn to start all over again.

Nunzio was fearless. One day he and Mike stacked two old rusty bedsprings on the ground and jumped on them from the top of the barn. Nunzio bounced and rolled and hurt himself. He screamed in terrible pain but soon pulled himself together and did it again!

Sometime later in the day, Mike's screams interrupted our happy play. "Slats is on the tractor and he can't get off." he hollered. "Somebody get Pop!"

We had nicknamed Nunzio "Slats" because he looked like one of the comic characters in the Saturday paper, *Abby and Slats*. Somehow Nunzio, who was then twelve, had started Mr. Desarmeau's tractor and couldn't stop it from moving. We ran to the east field and saw Slats riding the tractor in circles. His frantic, high-pitched screams could barely be heard above the roar of the motor. "I can't stop! I can't stop it! Somebody help!"

"Slats! Slats!" we yelled, running around the crusty field as we tried to save our brother from the runaway tractor. He couldn't or wouldn't release his grip from the wheel. We ran alongside with outstretched arms as if we could corner the beast, but mostly ended up dodging the tractor as it turned in circles. Headlights bounced up and down while the tractor revved its way across the rutted, hardened field. Nunzio kept going around in circles, crossing right hand over his left, continually turning the wheel.

Frank broke from the group and sprinted across the field hollering, "Pop! Pop! Come quick! The tractor won't stop," as if the thing had a mind of its own. "It's running all around the place!"

Suddenly, Nunzio straightened the wheel, stood up from the metal tractor seat, pressed the accelerator even harder, and headed straight for the ditch.

"Turn the wheel the other way; turn the wheel!" Mike shouted.

Nunzio, however, couldn't hear anything. He remained fixed on the fast-approaching ditch ahead of him, eyes wide open and mouth agape. Why he suddenly decided to hold the wheel straight, I'll never know. But as the tractor continued menacingly across the ruts toward the ditch, Nunzio suddenly leapt from the tractor as if he were Superman flying in the air with cameras rolling. He rolled on the ground several times and then lay still on his back. The tractor, meanwhile, continued on its doomed path. The front wheels ran down the slope of the ditch and, in a flash, stopped.

Kaboom!

The tractor crashed headfirst and we watched, captivated, as it slowly but surely turned over on its side, the wheels spinning with the motor still revving. Running and panting, I reached Nunzio first. I kneeled on the cold, mud-crusted field and laid both hands on him.

"Slats! Slats! Are you alright?"

He lay still, dazed and in tears.

"Ow," he said. "It hurts!"

Mike and the rest of the clan were right behind me. Mike and Louie lifted Nunzio and half-carried him, his hair askew, his face muddy, his pants torn at the knee.

"Don't tell Pop!" he cried and moaned, limping across the empty field. "Promise you won't tell Pop."

Of course it was too late. Pop had Frankie in tow when we saw him running towards us hollering, "What the hell did you kids do now?"

Slats quickly stood straight and tall and pushed us aside as Pop jumped into the ditch, bent down on one knee, and assessed the damage. He turned off the headlights and the ignition, but the wheels kept spinning.

"*Managia miseria!*" he screamed, swearing in Italian. Whenever he was extremely mad, Pop couldn't find the right words in English. "Did I not tell you boys not to touch this tractor? Well, did I? Did I?"

We sadly stood by as he stared at the dented tractor.

"Get in the house, all of you! Get moving!"

We were shell-shocked and remained frozen in place like soldiers on a smoking battlefield. Pop stood up and made like General Patton.

"Come on! Move it! Move it! Move it!" He took long strides and we ran behind him trying to keep pace, each one of us blurting, "It wasn't me, Pop! It wasn't me, Pop!"

Back at the house we assumed the usual lineup—all suspects under the threat of Pop's militaristic discipline. As always, he straddled a kitchen chair backwards, panting and glaring in exasperation. *Boy oh boy*, I thought, *Slats is gonna get it good this time!*

"I want to know which one of you flipped Mr. Desarmeau's tractor!" Pop wagged his finger in our faces.

No one spoke.

With his sharp observational skills, my father always knew when we were lying. He paid attention to how we sounded, watching for the telltale signs of deception, and tailored his approach to each of us individually. Then we observed the rapid flicking of his angered tongue.

"Tell me who did it, or else you'll all get it!"

The clock showed that it was only five o'clock. This looked to be another evening of no supper and strict orders to go directly to bed.

Nunzio inadvertently showed his true colours. He ran his fingers through his crew cut a number of times, a habit he had when agitated, revealing his guilt.

Pop was the best polygraph examiner in the world, and this was all he needed. His detection skills needed no tune-up.

"Why do you always look at me when something's wrong?" Nunzio said. "Why don't you look at somebody else for a change?"

My father's squinted eyes burned right through him. Rising from the rickety chair, he swung his leg and kicked the chair leg, pushing it to the centre of the room. Pop tilted his fedora back on his head and gave that steely-eyed look, his lips pursed.

Oh, how we dreaded that look.

"What did you say to me?"

Everyone held their breath. That one push of the fedora off his forehead told the story of what was to come.

"Stand at attention when I'm talking to you!"

Pop walked closer to Nunzio, his jaw flexing and teeth gritting, and he was breathing heavily. He suspected Nunzio but wasn't yet fully convinced. He slowly unhooked the buckle of his thick leather army belt, sliding it carefully and deliberately through each loop. The buckle fishtailed after each decisive move, a delay tactic he used to give the culprit responsible for the deed the opportunity to own up to his misdeed.

In a rare moment of weakness, Mike blurted out, "Nunzio, tell him you did it. You'd better tell him because I'm not getting a licking for nothing."

Most times we were unwavering in our support for one another, but now the floodgates had opened and everyone chimed in, "Yeah, we're not getting a licking for you. Tell him!"

"Shut up, Mike," Slats hissed, shifting his weight from one foot to the other as the verbal fireworks began under his breath.

"I'm not taking it for you, "Mike repeated.

"You shut up or I'll get you when we get back outside!" Nunzio answered. He swiped his crew cut once more with his right hand.

"Nunzio, step forward!" Pop commanded.

Nunzio, his hair tousled, broke from the line facing Pop. He looked like he had been in a cyclone. Matted clumps of grass and dirt hung from his favourite sweater, red and green with images of prancing reindeer and fluffy snowflakes that he had received courtesy of the Salvation Army box the year before.

"Why did you go near that tractor when I told you over and over not to?" Pop demanded. "And you'd better tell the truth!"

Nunzio swallowed hard. The hush in the house made it a quiet tomb. "It was an accident," he blubbered. "I was just sitting there on the seat pretending to drive it. I pushed some buttons and it started all by itself. I touched the gears and the tractor moved. I swear I didn't mean to drive the tractor, Pop." Tears overflowed as he choked on his words. We all hoped for a quick end.

"Do you think I have money to pay for this damage? Look around you! This could get us kicked out."

Nunzio cried even harder.

"You're going to pay for this. You're going to work for Mr. Desarmeau after school every day and on weekends too, until he says it's enough. That's what you're going to do."

"But I'm only twelve," Nunzio blurted. "I don't want to work for him! He's a slave driver!"

Pop's temper exploded and he jumped up and yanked the belt from the remaining loop. He grabbed Slats by the arm to whip his bottom, but Nunzio darted ahead and the belt buckle struck him across the back of his legs. Pop pursued and struck him a second time before Nunzio escaped. Pop caught him again, and walloped him across the backside four or five more times with the leather.

The rest of us stood very still, afraid to breathe, hoping Pop's wrath would not spill over to the rest of us as it often did. After all, we were all guilty by association. Then the telltale look from

Louie signalled for us to make a run for it. We bolted up the stairs, crammed into one room, and cringed on the bed as still as mice. With the threat ever present, Sam, eight, instinctively rolled under the bed and hoped to go unnoticed. Sometimes this worked and Pop would forget about one or another of us.

A long time later, we heard Pop wringing out a cloth in a water basin. Pat and Vince tiptoed across the hallway and halfway down the stairs. Once he calmed down, Pop would come to his senses, and though still stern, he would feel bad for the corporal punishment he had dished out. The boys crept further down a few steps, holding their breath. Pop was nursing the welts on Nunzio's legs.

"You could have been killed on that tractor, son," he gently said. Nunzio sobbed in muffled tones. I knew that Pop was weeping, too, if only on the inside.

We waited a little longer for things to cool down, but eventually hunger pangs got the better of Pat. He peeked out and said, "Could we have something to eat now, Pop?"

Troubled by the physical injury he'd inflicted on Nunzio, Pop said, "Come and get it. And I don't want to hear a peep out of any of you. You eat and then you go to bed."

Somewhat relieved, we went downstairs and shared furtive looks with one another while we ate. None of us said a word.

Year after year, we survived the punishments resulting from Nunzio's grand curiosity, Louie's mischief and Frank's devilish play. During those years, we built our own support system by remaining close friends. We forged a powerful loyalty among us, a trait that was vital to surviving the effects of growing up in a large family where, any day, at any time, any crazy thing could and did happen.

Nunzio worked all summer for Mr. Desarmeau to repay the damages to the tractor.

On Sundays

On Sundays, we slept in—until 6:30 a.m.

Every Sunday morning, my father walked between the beds and shook each of our shoulders until we stirred. Most of us snuggled right back under the stack of Salvation Army coats covering us. Once the coal stove died out during the night, the chilly house drove us deeper into the stained mattresses and under those coats.

"Come on, boys. It's six-thirty and you've gotta get up. Hup, two, three!" Pop labelled all of us boys; gender didn't matter. "You're in the army now!"

I held my breath and remained hidden under the covers.

"Just a little bit longer," we always begged. The words formed frosty clouds in the arctic air.

"It's a long walk to church," he warned. "You have to get up... hup, two, three!"

"Why does he treat us like soldiers?" I said to my younger brother, Pat. "We're just kids."

Pat was curled in the fetal position next to me with a toque on his head. At the foot of the bed Frankie screamed, "Vince, get your feet out of my face! They stink!"

Every winter during the vicious cold, we closed off one side of the drafty clapboard farmhouse. Two double beds were crammed into each bedroom, and four kids negotiated for a place in each bed. We all wanted to sleep next to our brother or sister closest in age so we could talk quietly after my father blew out the lantern. Night after night, the same words were whispered across the room.

"Get to sleep up there or I'll come up and put you to sleep!"

On Sunday mornings, we slipped into as many layers of clothing as we could find and my father helped with the final touches.

"Here, put these socks on your hands under your mittens. Is everyone's feet wrapped? Gus, did you take care of your sister?"

Pop then knelt down and checked our feet. Often, he removed my rubber boots and rewrapped the newspaper tighter around my feet so they slipped into my boots with ease.

One Sunday, when he discovered we were short a scarf or two, he tore up one of his Department of Highways shirts and tied it around Sammy's face and forehead, leaving only his eyes exposed. Once he had us properly bundled up, our father marched us down the road to St. Mary's Church. After trudging through the snow for an hour, we arrived at the church, some of us in tears, and waited for my father to remove the mittens and socks and rub our hands with his giant hands that were as warm as a heater.

Pop pointed to the pews as we walked into the church and commanded, "Louie, Mike and Nunzio, over there. Pat and Marie, you sit here with me. Sammy, Frank and Vince, go with your older brother. Remember, I'm sitting behind you. No pushing, no shoving, no fighting and no talking. Be quiet and pay close attention to what Father Tompkins says."

We saw him in this mode many times before and understood the punishment for misbehaving in church, which included a quick kick in the rear or a swift smack on the head.

"Yes, Pop," we said and nodded in acknowledgement. But the promise was soon forgotten as we fought for the precious end seats.

We learned not to care so much when people pointed fingers at our large brood. When Father Tompkins paused during mass and craned his neck to peer into the crowd from the high pulpit, the congregation always turned around to see from whence came the rumblings of noise interrupting the mass. It was usually us.

Everyone turned and gawked at my father and what they saw made us laugh—head bowed, arms folded, spectacles resting on the end of his nose, prayer book fallen to the floor, Pop was cutting some ear-splitting snores. His church nap gave us licence to shove, elbow and jostle for aisle seats, whispering and talking to each other with impunity. At least until we got home.

Once home, our Sunday breakfast consisted of a bowl of tomato sauce with two large meatballs and several slices of bread. We helped Pop roll two hundred meatballs every Saturday and placed them into the huge cauldron of sauce for our Sunday breakfast and Sunday pasta dinner. Those Sunday meals, more than any other meal, satisfied us and nourished our bodies as much as Pop had hoped the service would save our souls.

The Harvest

We were quite settled on the farm in Marvelville. Every other Saturday night, we jammed the evenings away with Pop playing his new accordion. Along with our favourites, we also sang Italian songs such as "Eh, Cumpare!" "Santa Lucia" and "O Sole Mio." When Pop yelled, "Get in the circle, boys," we scraped the chairs against the bare wooden floor, pushing them back against the wall to make room for dancing.

"Frankie, you're my partner," I said, hooking his arm in delight. Frankie was three years younger and I easily swung him around and around and off his feet.

The radio weatherman that fall and the *Farmers' Almanac* had forecast a long, harsh winter. Farmers were anxious to get their crops in. The harvest was more pressing than school, socials— everything. Everyone in the community understood the need to pull children out of the classroom to pick the potatoes and turnips. Our large family had a widespread reputation for being hard workers, and farmers were eager to hire us kids. This interrupted the Saturday night sing-a-longs and dances that we so enjoyed.

As we prepared to leave home to gather the first crop, Pop told Gus, "Look after your brothers, and especially your sister, Marie.

She's the only girl going, so you take care of her. Remember, you're the oldest, and all of you"—he pointed at us—"watch your manners and listen to your older brother or else you're gonna get it when you get back."

Six of my brothers and I resided with different farmers for one or two weeks at a stretch, depending on the farmer's yield, until all the crops were in. Five other siblings were too young and stayed home, and four older ones lived and worked in the city.

Gus, fifteen and the eldest living at home, drove Pop's 1937 DeSoto. If you were tall enough to reach the pedals of any car or tractor on the farm, then you were old enough to drive on the back roads. We were all one year apart in age. Vince was nine; Pat, ten; I was eleven; Nunzio, twelve; Mike, thirteen; and Lou, fourteen.

"Okay, let's go!" Gus hollered. "Get in the car."

Lou and Mike elbowed their way into the car as they scrambled to get the front seat, the rest of us climbed in, and off we rode to Angus O'Rourke's farm. Under the full supervision of the notorious farmer, the two dollars we earned each day wasn't anywhere near fair, considering the strenuous labour he demanded. He drove us like he drove his team of huge horses that pulled the potato digger. Other than lunchtime, Mr. O'Rourke allowed us only two five-minute breaks—one in the morning and one in the afternoon. His fields stretched far beyond our sight under the sweltering sun.

"You can't stop for water until we reach the end of a row," he said, not wanting to lose time. An ice-cold bucket of well water placed beyond our reach created a cruel incentive for us. Even when we were permitted to pause for a drink of the water, he kept driving the team hard and we had to race to keep up.

One day, beet red and sweaty, Lou and Gus had had enough. "We're not his slaves!" Gus said. "He can piss off! Just watch.

Hand me that big rock, Lou. I'll fix him." Wagging his finger at us, Gus said, "Don't any of you say a word."

Lou picked up the rock with both hands and carried it between his legs. As Mr. O'Rourke snapped the reigns of the horses, Gus took the rock from Lou, lifted it over his head, and heaved it with both hands into the digger. It ground to a halt.

Mr. O'Rourke pulled the reins, calling, "Whoa, whoa!" The team danced on their hoofs and came to a standstill. He climbed down from the digger, cleared it with his hands, and kicked the dirt with his boots. "Goddamn piece of shit, this machine!" he fumed and cursed. "Somethun's always wrong!"

He climbed back up on his seat, grabbed the reins, and cracked the whip. He pressed his tongue to the roof of his mouth, pursed his lips, and gave the familiar "clicking" commands to the team. The horses sprang forward at the piercing sting of the reins on their backs. Stretching hardened muscles, they plunged their heads toward the ground and pulled the digger, burrowing it through the dry, crusty soil and forcing the darkened earth to open up like a zipper as it scratched out tons of potatoes.

As Mr. O'Rourke focused on the long stretch ahead of him, the boys forced many of the loose potatoes back into the softened ground with the heels of their boots, closing the distance between the team and us.

One night as we turned in, Mr. O'Rourke told a neighbouring farmer in the kitchen, "Boy, I can really drive those *Eyetie* kids."

The boys dropped to their knees and peered down through the cracks in the floorboards as the two men talked in hushed tones about us.

"They're harder workers than any kids I've ever had," Mr. O'Rourke continued. "They work no matter how hard I drive them."

Lou raised his head back up. In anger, he pounded his fist silently on the floor.

Within two weeks, Mr. O'Rourke's potato harvest had been brought in. Wetting his thumb with his tongue, he slowly counted out twenty-eight dollars for each of us, two dollars per day for two weeks.

"Well now, don't you kids forget, I want you back here again next year, you hear?"

"Yes, Mr. O'Rourke," we chorused obediently, throwing not-if-we-can-help-it looks at each other.

We gathered our sweaters and jackets and headed to the car. Once out of earshot, Nunzio said, "Go to hell, Angus O'Rourke."

"Hey," Lou said. "What do you say we snatch up some chickens on the way out?"

"Yeah, let's steal some chickens," Mike said. "Let's do it!"

The thought of a chicken dinner, unaffordable in our home, made Lou smack his lips. He rubbed his tummy and with widened eyes said, "Yum-yum, we're gonna have chicken on Sunday!"

"Okay, let's get going," Gus said and shoved us into the car.

Nunzio and Vince flanked Pat and I in the back seat; Gus and Lou sat on each side of Mike in the front. Hunched over the steering wheel, Gus coasted quietly down the long gravel driveway. The chickens waddled idly by, paying no mind to the car.

"When I say so," Gus instructed, "everybody grab a chicken."

Seconds later we heard, "Okay, now! Go!"

In a single movement, the four car doors opened. Vince and Nunzio leaned out, holding onto the car's frame with one hand, while Gus held onto the steering wheel. From the front seat, Lou caught a chicken by the leg with his free hand, and Gus got another in one quick swoop. From the back seat, Vince held his chicken's beak closed, muffling its loud squawking. Lou passed his chicken to Mike seated next to him, and then managed to quickly scoop up another. Each chicken we grabbed trumpeted our joy. The car doors slammed shut. Gus floored it and we bounced up and down on the worn shocks along the driveway, leaving behind a cloud of dust.

"To hell with Mr. O'Rourke!" Lou called to us in the back seat.

After each crop, we checked in at home briefly, handed the money over to Pop, then moved on to the next farm. This time Pop asked, "Where did you get the chickens?"

"Oh, Mr. O'Rourke gave us the chickens for our extra-hard work," Gus said quickly.

Pop glowed with fatherly pride.

We next drove to the Spratt family farm. At breakfast on the first morning, we came downstairs at seven o'clock to a table set with an egg in an eggcup and an egg at the side of each plate. We poked each other in the ribs looking at the food. Vince beamed with a wide grin. "Wow, hard-boiled eggs," he said and raced to grab a seat at the table.

Once a year, at Easter, we feasted on eggs. Pop always boiled one hundred and forty-four eggs, hiding them in and around the house and barn for us to find. He left obvious "hints," like eggs peeking out from mounds of straw.

Vince picked up his egg from the cup and banged it on the table, cracking the shell to peel. Two seconds behind him, we did the same. Egg yolk ran everywhere.

"What the hell!" Vince said. "Raw eggs!"

We had never seen a soft-boiled egg before. Gus grabbed the kitchen cloth from the sink and started to clean up the mess. Mrs. Spratt threw us a stern glance as she poured herself a cup of coffee. She was not accustomed to having seven young children in her home and seemed annoyed by every move we made.

She picked up her spoon, gently tapped the top of her egg several times, peeled the crown, and then dipped her spoon into the soft yolk.

We picked up our spoons and, in silence, copied her.

"So," said Mr. Spratt, wiping his mouth with the back of his hand after slurping the last of his tea and then tilting the wooden chair on its back legs, "I hear you kids are good workers. Well, let's get to it. Twenty acres of potatoes won't pick themselves. There'll be no stopping till the work's done."

We sighed.

"Another guy who thinks we're horses," Nunzio muttered.

Once out of earshot, we mocked Mr. Spratt. We moved our heads side to side, squinted and puckered our faces, and said over and over again, "Twenty acres of potatoes won't pick themselves! Twenty acres of potatoes won't pick themselves!"

We slept in the attic when we worked at the Spratt farm, where they kept two large round top trunks containing theatrical costumes and swords. While the Spratts slept, we dressed in the costumes and played pirates, swashbuckling our way onto imaginary pirate ships and stealing glorious treasures. We jumped from bed to bed, swords flailing, whispering, "Har-har" and "Aye, Ca-pi-tan."

Mr. Spratt was no better than Mr. O'Rourke and drove us from sunup to sundown, breaking ground and picking potatoes. Every night, our backs ached, but we didn't let this stop us from having some fun. Each night, we tiptoed across the wide hallway, past the Spratt's bedroom. Gus would press his finger to his lips to silence us as we crept down the stairs to take our revenge. We would raid the fridge and eat everything in sight.

On the fourth night, we sneaked down to raid the fridge once more, but found it under padlock and key!

A week and a half later, after a quick stop home, we moved on to the farm of Mr. and Mrs. Desarmeau. Standing in her doorway, hands on her hips, Mrs. Desarmeau, like all the others before her, scanned us—seven ragged children—with a large measure of disdain. Then her eyes stopped at Pat's bare feet.

"Where are your shoes, child?" she asked.

"I threw them away," Pat said.

"Whatever for?"

"They were too big for me and they kept falling off my feet. They made me trip."

"But you need shoes," she said. "The thistles and sharp rocks will cut your feet."

"I don't want them," Pat said.

"On such a chilly fall day, you'll need to have shoes in the fields and that's that," she said and then turned to Mr. Desarmeau and muttered, "Where the hell did you find this lot?"

Mrs. Desarmeau walked over to the hall closet and frantically dug into boxes, sending items flying into the hallway behind her.

"Aha!" she finally said, holding out a pair of old lady heels. She handed them to Pat.

"Put them on," she said. "It's better than nothing."

We started laughing hysterically.

"I don't want those shoes!" Pat cried.

"Put them on," she yelled, then raised Pat's foot and forced on a shoe.

We all doubled over with laughter, pointing and screeching at Pat.

Mrs. Desarmeau noticed Pat didn't have a hat, either. She grabbed a tea towel from the rack by the woodstove, placed it on his head, and tied it under his chin like a kerchief. Now we laughed and screeched even harder, gasping and coughing for air.

Mrs. Desarmeau, inflamed by our antics, pushed her hand into Nunzio's back.

"All of you, march!" she ordered. "Follow me to the fields."

We walked right behind her and tried to stifle our laughter each time she turned around and glared at us.

Every day in the fields we pointed our fingers and chanted, "Ha-ha, Pat! You look like an old lady!"

Two weeks later, we completed the harvest at the Desarmeau's, our last farm for the summer, and returned home.

"Pop, we're home," we screamed as we piled out of the car after having been away for six weeks with only a few hour-long visits home.

I stared into my father's clear hazel eyes and fixed on the deep lines in his forehead. He looked different. I hadn't noticed before that his eyes were hazel. His moustache looked thinner, and the lines deeper. He opened his arms and gathered in as many of us as he could.

"Let me look at you!" he said. "Thank God you're home safe and sound! I hope you all behaved yourselves and didn't shame me."

At the kitchen table, we counted the money. Each of us divided our earnings into two piles, half for Pop to help out with food for the family and half for us to buy candy, school exercise books, pencils, shoes, and whatever else we wanted or needed to buy. Pat ran to the outhouse, got the old Eaton's catalogue that doubled as toilet paper, and we thumbed our way through it.

We handed the bills over to our father and kept all the change because it looked like a lot more money. We fondled the coins. They felt so good in our hands. We traded newer coins for older ones, and older ones for newer ones, and shiny ones for dull ones. Every day, we counted the pennies, the nickels, the dimes and the quarters, stacking them over and over, figuring out how much we'd have left over for candy after we had bought shoes and school supplies.

My older brothers and sisters, Steve and Phil and Caroline and Josephine, had come home from the city to visit as they usually did on Saturdays. With all his children together in one place, Pop pulled out his accordion. The boys scurried for their instruments. The familiar sound of scraping chairs across the barn board floor was heard and sixteen excited kids manoeuvred for position. Squeaky notes soared from the cherished accordion while Pop hummed and fanned, trying to find the right key. With heads bent over their guitars and Lou over his banjo, the boys tuned their strings with big, wide grins. Their looping hands and arms persuaded song and dance out of their instruments, and the rest of us kids swung each other off our feet.

The evening toned down and my older siblings headed back to the city. Then we went to bed exhausted but happy.

The Confessional

In the early 1950s, thanks to the help of my older siblings who held jobs, we were finally able to afford electricity for the house.

Steve came home one weekend and set up a small black and white television set with rabbit ears.

On Saturday nights, it became our custom to watch *Hockey Night in Canada*. One of the boys had to stand beside the TV and slam it whenever wavy lines or snowy images appeared. My father loved hockey, and he could not stand any interference. The boys also loved hockey and whoever's turn it was to whack the TV hated the job because he could only view the game from a severe angle.

We also watched *The Ed Sullivan Variety Show* every Sunday night. Senor Wences, a ventriloquist who kept a dummy in a box, was a frequent guest. He spoke to the dummy on and off as he opened and closed the box.

Upon opening the box Senor Wences, in a Spanish accent, would stretch the word "yes" and say to the dummy, "Yessss? Hello?" And the dummy would reply, "It's aright; close de box," or alternatively, "Open de box!"

The opening and closing of the box and the mirrored response of the dummy threw us into knee-slapping fits of laughter, producing tears. Sometimes, it was difficult for us to catch our breath.

———

Sam, now eight, sat pruned and groomed waiting patiently in the darkened confessional. He wore his Sunday best—white shirt buttoned to the neck, sharply creased dress pants and shoes polished to a mirror-like high lustre. His shiny, coal-black hair, coached into a mounded wave, added several inches to his height.

In the pew next to the confessional, Vince, ten, and Pat, nine, sat, their hair crested with the same great wave, wearing the identical outfit, earmarked only for church on Sundays or other special occasions such as baptisms, communions, confirmations or house parties.

Every Saturday, my twelve-year-old hands ironed all the white shirts and pressed all the pants to a sharp line as instructed by Pop for my eight brothers still living at home. In the morning, the very thought of this task gave me stooped shoulders and heavy feet the entire day. I didn't understand why I had to be a slave to the boys.

Two heavy cast irons sat side by side on the woodstove and radiated intense heat that, alas, allowed me to work uninterrupted. I toiled for hours over those blistering irons. When one iron cooled, I slipped it back onto the stovetop and picked up the other. The hot iron hissed and sputtered and scorched the dampened, shredded tea towel laid overtop the garment, as I glided it across the fabric and smoothed out all wrinkles.

Before confession on Sunday mornings, the usual consultation and comparison of notes took place about who would confess what. We did not embrace weekly confessions but, rather, endured them. As good Catholics, they were of course mandatory. But to us, mandatory meant telling our confessions by rote. There was no artfulness to our confessions, no surprises, and they went like this: "Bless me Father for I have sinned. It's been one week since my last confession. I fought with my brother. I took the Lord's name in vain. I had hateful thoughts about my father after he hit me."

Whew. Then it was all over.

Father instructed atonement. "Say the whole Rosary, add two Hail Marys, one Our Father and one Glory Be."

Week after week we knelt and made amends. As Sunday rolled around, thinking about what we'd confess during the upcoming confession or what far-out story we could resurrect irked us. Never really understanding weekly confessions nor seeing the good they did, we felt the real confessions were found with the experienced sinners. Our childish crimes were petty and not worth repeating to anyone.

An austere no-nonsense priest, Father Tompkins wore his wire-rimmed reading glasses on the tip of his nose so that he could look over the frame. Somehow, this seemed to add an extra layer of disapproval to his demeanor. His eyes were a kaleidoscope of blue flecked with purple and gold around the edges. His grey hair complemented his perpetually rosy cheeks. In later years, I wondered about the source of that rosy bloom!

Looming over us and in a heavy-handed voice, he would say, "Did you do your penance last week?"

Transformed little respectful saints that we were, we would reply in unison, "Yes we did, Father; thank you, Father," and then scamper away before he could burden us with more prayers.

As I knelt in the church pew saying my penance, I heard Father Tompkins slide open the lattice window of the confessional to hear Sam's confession. I cocked my head to hear the whispers of

Sam's sins. I heard Father Tompkins say, "Yes, my son?" putting a long drawl on the word *yes*.

Sam giggled. We knew immediately that he was thinking of Senor Wences opening and closing "de box."

Within seconds, Sam's muffled giggles escalated into uncontrollable all-out laughter. He tried to muffle the sound, but his laughter kept breaking out from behind his hand on his mouth. Vince and Pat shrieked and before you knew it, they all had tears running down their cheeks. Try as they might, they just couldn't smother the sounds.

I heard the boom and echo of the small lattice confessional window slam shut. Father Tompkins blazed out of the confessional, nostrils flaring, huffing and puffing. He grabbed Sam by the back of his shirt collar and dragged him on his heels to the pew, throwing him beside Vince and Pat. His voice reverberated throughout the stained-glass church.

"If you can't behave like civilized people, get out of my church! I'm going to report this to your father!"

Father Tompkins always held us in holy fear, and our laughter stopped dead.

The priest passed us in his car as we walked home from church on the dusty dirt road. We knew he was flaming mad and would reach Pop before we did. He often stopped to give some of us a ride when he happened upon us walking. But on this day, he left a puff of dust whirling around behind him. We dilly-dallied home, kicking pebbles along the way, anything to delay the impending reprimand. Father Tompkins's sphere of influence stretched far and wide with the parishioners.

When we reached the house, Pop stood in the doorway with fire in his wide eyes. "Laugh at the priest, will you?" he said, before we had a chance to speak. "I'll teach you to laugh at the priest!"

He smacked Pat and Sam and then knuckled them over the head—they later said they could count the number of knuckles he used by the amount of pressure that came down on them—and then kicked them in the rear and sent them to their room. Those hard knuckles over the head hurt something fierce, and everyone tried to run away as fast as the hand that came down. There were some things Pop wouldn't tolerate you poking fun at and one of them was a priest. To ridicule a priest was sacrilege. You also did not mock the teacher, the doctor, and least of all, your father.

Pop sometimes overheard us mimicking Father Tompkins while we pretended that Sam and Pat were back in the confessional with the opening and closing of the box. He would give us a quiet, cold look, and we stopped immediately.

Now, as adults, my siblings and I often recount these stories about Father Tompkins and cry out in absolute fits of laughter and screech with delight. They still make us laugh until the tears come.

Opera Comes Into My Life

Every Saturday afternoon, from the age of twelve, I heard the infallible strains of Verdi's *Rigoletto* or *La Traviata,* Mozart's *Marriage of Figaro,* or Bizet's *Carmen,* the timeless story of Don Jose and his doomed love for a local gypsy woman.

My father made us watch these Saturday afternoon operas on our second hand black and white television that had spindly aluminum legs and sat against the back wall.

My brothers hated opera with a passion, and on Saturday afternoons, the minute Pop fell under the hypnotic spell of the music, they tiptoed out behind his back and raced from the room. My love of opera came slowly and steadily, beginning when I heard the first notes of the haunting cantata of Offenbach's *Barcarolle* and Carmen's *Habanera.* Pop helped navigate me through the words and movements as I became enthralled by the elaborate costumes and impossibly high-pitched voices. I cherished my time alone with Pop as we sat, lost in the haunted cantata of Puccini's *Madame Butterfly,* enchanted by the supreme efforts of the sopranos and tenors who bared their souls.

Pop dearly loved music of all types. At our house parties, he took centre stage and belted out "O Sole Mio" and "Return to Sorrento" in a vibrato not challenged by many.

Mostly, though, our family listened to country and western music on the one local radio station that did not have static. I liked country and western music, but my brothers loved it. Four of them—Pat, Louie, Gus and Vince—became self-taught guitarists. They listened and played along to Eddy Arnold singing cowboy songs or Ernest Tubb's crying-in-your-beer songs or the famous Canadian western singer from Alberta, Wilf Carter.

On Saturday nights, if there wasn't a hockey game on, we pushed the kitchen chairs against the wall. Pat, Gus, Louie and Vince picked up their guitars. My father strapped on his weathered, well-used accordion and coaxed the pleats in and out, lending his ear to the keys to test the sound. Then a chorus of fourteen voices resonated throughout the farmhouse, singing, "When the moon hits your eye like a big pizza pie, that's amore," or "Lazy Mary will you get up? She answered back, 'I am not able.' Lazy Mary would you get up? We need the sheets for the table." We all linked arms, singing and swaying with all our might next to the fire in the potbelly stove, which sparked and danced along with us.

Pop instilled in us an appreciation for all music, but opera was his first love. I liked watching the expression on Pop's face as he listened to the exquisite melodies. He would close his eyes and scrunch his shoulders like he was sipping hot tea on a cold winter's eve, and breathe deeply, slowly stretching his neck to the heavens as if in some strange, wonderful trance. He looked as if he had been touched by an angel.

Pop and his service medals

Remembrance Day

Every Remembrance Day, my father gathered my siblings and me in his bedroom one hour before 11 a.m. to honour his fallen comrades from World War I and World War II.

My oldest sister told me that she and my two older brothers had once accompanied Pop to Remembrance Day services at Confederation Square in Ottawa where he joined in the march with the other soldiers. She said that he had forgotten to bring his army jacket. After arriving at the Square, he still marched in the biting-cold ceremony without the jacket. When we were old enough to understand, and when there were too many of us kids to load in the car, we had our own ceremony each year at home.

On one memorable chilly winter morning on November 11th, eight or nine of us, as usual, formed a circle on the cold, wooden floor in Pop's bedroom. I squeezed in from the outer fringe of the group, forcing the circle to open up a tiny bit wider on the cold floor. We sat cross-legged according to rank in age: Louie, Mike, Nunzio and then me, Pat, Vince, Frank and finally Sam.

My younger siblings were far too young to fathom the impact of Pop's war stories, so they were not permitted in the bedroom, and played downstairs instead.

Prominently displayed in one corner of the room, my father kept a heavy brown steamer trunk which guarded the objects Pop held sacred and dear: immigration papers, family photos, my mother's wedding ring, her heart-shaped locket and the meagre life insurance policies he was able to afford for each of his children. But the most interesting items to us were Pop's WWI gas mask, his army helmet, a single discharged bullet housed in a glass jar, a bayonet, and a German Lugar handgun my father had taken from a dead German soldier in the trenches. A splendid, colourful array of red, white and blue, gold, and green and purple ribboned service medals also found a home in the trunk.

My mother had been dead for several years now, but rumour had it that she had lain awake many nights dreading receipt of the telegram sent to the families of soldiers killed or missing in action. She waited for my father to return home, and with the help of my older siblings, she managed all of us alone during those years.

Pop knelt in front of the trunk and tenderly caressed the ancient wood as if he were gently smoothing the wrinkles on his bed. Then, as he did each year, he briskly unsnapped the metal clasps to survey his treasures of honour and glory.

Gliding his hand over the articles, he stopped when he touched the glass jar holding the single bullet that had been removed from his left arm, and absentmindedly ran his hand along the scar on his left shoulder. He looked past us with that thousand-yard stare and barked, "Private First Class Marini reporting for duty, Sir!"

Pulling his shoulders back smartly, he snapped his hand to his forehead in a perfect salute.

"Tell us about the bullet, Daddy!"

"Tell us about when you were shot!"

"Did it hurt?"

"Tell us about the fighting!"

"Tell us how they carried you off on the stretcher!"

"Boys!" Pop said sternly and we all fell silent. "Battalions of men, boys really, all in their teens or twenties, never made it back home."

We stared into his fierce eyes riveted, as always, by this captivating story. He pulled out the bayonet. I covered my face and peeked out at him through trembling fingers, knowing he was going to test the sharpness of the blade. He ran his thumb along its razor-sharp edge. All eyes were on Pop.

"Hand-to-hand combat, boys," he said, his voice deep and raspy, almost a whisper. "We fixed our bayonets on the end of our rifles and said a prayer to God in heaven that they wouldn't be turned against us."

I dropped my hands, eyes wide, fascinated, fear in my heart.

"Hearts pounded like hammers...boom, boom, boom." He struck his fist against his chest. "Then we ran toward the enemy, and they toward us, and the air was filled with the ear-piercing roar of battle."

With a swift graceful gesture, Pop turned the bayonet forward, as if ready to charge. "Before I knew it, it was all over in a field of blood, a battlefield like I had never imagined in all my days," he said. "The shells burned like lightning and the earth shook like thunder, and only the fortunate remained."

We had all leaned so far in at this point in the story that if someone had grazed our backs with a feather we would have all fallen into a pile on the floor at Pop's feet. As my father told his stories of the war and the uphill charges, we sat, mirroring each other's expressions—mouths agape, eyebrows raised, absorbed in every single word he said, and eager for more.

"We were stuck for days on end in the trenches, boys. And every day it was the same—heavy shelling, grenades. Hell itself had been unleashed on Earth from a thousand different directions."

"Were you scared, Pop?" asked one of my younger brothers in a small voice.

"Was I scared? We were all scared. We were so scared we didn't sleep. Men were bound more closely to each other than to members of their own family. We were family!"

Pop grew quiet, remembering his fallen comrades. We stared at him, hushed. Pop was our hero.

"All my friends are gone now," he said sadly. "Sometimes, in my dreams, I see my old chum, Jimmy. I'm in the trenches, the fog rolls in and a lone soldier comes trudging through the mist. 'Jimmy!' I shout and jump up to greet him. 'I'm so glad you're all right!' Then I hear a shot. I wake up. The medics carry me off to the field hospital and my arm is limp and bloody beside me."

As he sat open-mouthed, Louie whispered, "When I grow up, I want to be a soldier just like you, Daddy."

Mike piped up a little louder, "Me too, Daddy! I want to be a soldier, too!"

"Me too!" yelled Vince.

There was no way that I wanted to be a soldier, what with being scared like that all the time. No siree!

Pop allowed each one of us to try on his helmet and hold his gun. He removed the bullet from the glass jar and placed it in Louie's hand. He examined it, and then passed it down the line, each of us awestruck.

Pop took out our mother's photograph from the trunk. Louie was the first to kiss it, as instructed by our father, but before releasing the photo, I noticed Pop stare at it for a long time.

We remained seated on the floor and marvelled at these valued possessions. Although we were only children, we understood our father's world of honour, regimen and discipline. After examining the memorabilia and passing the items around the circle, we headed to the parlour at two minutes before eleven and lined up again.

"Men, front and centre...hup, two, three!"

My father looked handsome with his perfectly trimmed Errol Flynn moustache and hazel eyes. The army hat on his head proudly displayed a poppy. His khaki army jacket didn't fit as well as before, but the display of shiny medals that hung from the colourful striped bar pinned over his heart gleamed like new patent leather, the multicoloured ribbons standing out like colourful balloons.

Pop walked up and down the line, hands clasped behind his back, and "inspected the troops." He licked his palm and flattened Vincent's cowlick, wet his thumb and erased a smudge on Mike's face, and he straightened little Sammy's shirt collar.

"Ah-ten-shun!"

A neat row of tiny soldiers snapped to attention like boot camp cadets.

"Bow your heads in honour of the men who gave their lives so that you could sleep under a cover of peace and freedom each night. Bow your heads for the men who gave up everything they would ever be, so that you could be anything you want to be. Never forget that. Never forget them."

We observed the moment in exquisite silence as our father began to cry unabashedly. As the tears lined his weary face, I could almost feel the lump in his throat in my own. Afraid to move before the time was up, we remained painfully still and quiet.

My father's show of emotion each Remembrance Day always touched me. At the time, I did not understand much of it, but it hurt me to see him cry. He was always a large man in stature and larger-than-life in spirit, and it pained me to see him so vulnerable and naked. My throat narrowed and tears spilled down my cheeks. I glanced at the wet faces of my older brothers.

"At ease, men," Pop finally said, breaking the thick silence and releasing us for the day. We were soon back outside, climbing trees and playing Cowboys and Indians, as was our routine.

On Remembrance Day evening, my father would command another circle next to the blazing fire in the potbelly stove and bring out his accordion, leading us into wartime songs. We knew all the words verbatim to such standards as "Lili Marlene," "Pack up Your Troubles in Your Old Kit Bag" and "This is the Army, Mr. Jones."

My father sang these wartime songs on a regular basis and his powerful tales always drew us in like moths to a flame. His words never bored us; they mattered to us. We breathed them in as we did the air, and I know he found this satisfying.

Those who returned, such as my father, kept alive the memories of those who did not. Every November 11th after my father died, his children carried on the sacred tradition of remembrance. I often became the dispatcher of the message to my brothers in Toronto that my father had instructed: "Don't forget what today means. Remember that moment of silence. Remember my friends who died for you."

I close my eyes and picture my father, just a boy himself, on the battlefield. He holds his rifle with both his hands, close to his body, bayonet forward, in the charge position. He runs forward through the muck and the mud. Each hard step gives way to splashes of dirty water and more mud. His face, dirty and battle-weary, shows the fear he so aptly demonstrated to us on those Remembrance Days.

The wars gave my father many deep friendships and profound experiences. He had seen the world change in ways that I would never witness, and he shared those changes with his children through his stories. He allowed us to see the world through his eyes.

As his young listeners, we imagined him climbing that hill, moving forward with a unit of young men, bayonets forward, charging the enemy. We saw our father as a gallant hero, a fearless soldier, and a comrade to his friends-in-arms without question. He was the High Commander of our family!

In a way, my father and his fellow soldiers found in each other what others seek their entire lives—a special kind of unity, an unbreakable bond, a brotherhood united for a common purpose. It came at great cost. They were ennobled in life, and brothers in death.

Canada Bread

The white powdered sugar on the mouths of my brothers enraged Pop. "So you *did* steal the doughnuts from the bread truck," he yelled. "I've told you a thousand times—never steal when we have enough to eat!"

Earlier that day, the boys had watched the bread truck rumble up the driveway with keen interest. "Canada Bread" in large white letters was painted on the side of the truck with the familiar wheat sheaf logo. "Wholesale Cakes" was pasted on the door. We knew heaven dwelled inside that truck.

Canada Bread stopped at our farm twice a week, leaving eighteen loaves of bread each time. At eighteen cents per loaf, the cost was over six dollars per week. Pop kept an account with the company. Every day for lunch, the boys each ate four sandwiches and I ate two.

On Mondays, Pop dished up meatball sandwiches made from the beef left over from the Sunday dinner. For the rest of the week, we ate peanut butter and jam sandwiches taken from the two-gallon pails purchased monthly. Sometimes, when the monthly food supply was depleted, we devoured white margarine spread between two slices of bread or mustard sandwiches with sugar sprinkled between two layers. During the fall, Pop purchased bushels of green peppers and with the eggs the stolen chickens produced, we ate scrambled egg and pepper sandwiches. Each one of us also scoffed down ten pieces of toast every morning with white margarine scraped on them. In all, thirty-six loaves of bread were devoured each week.

On this day, however, it wasn't bread my brothers had on their larcenous little minds. The bread man had left the rear doors of the delivery truck open for a crime of opportunity. While the bread man busied himself making trips into the house with trays of our bread, my brothers Gus, Louie and Mike formed an assembly line at the rear of the truck. Gus pitched out boxes of sugared doughnuts to Louie, who tossed them over the hedge to Mike, who tossed the boxes to the runner, Nunzio, who ran into the nearby bushes and hid them for later consumption. The plan worked perfectly until the bread man came back out after his final trip into the house. He walked to the back of the truck to close the doors. We held our breaths from our hiding places and prayed that we would hear those doors slam shut and the engine start.

But there was total silence. The bread man was looking into the rear of the truck as if he knew something was sideways but hadn't quite figured it out. Then the doors slammed a little too hard and I heard the voice of the Canada Bread man reverberate across the countryside.

"Little thieves!" he bellowed.

The bread man had figured it out. He stormed back to the house and confronted my father on the porch.

"Your kids stole doughnuts from my truck!"

Pop had a default belief that his offspring could do no wrong. He refused to listen to such nonsense and told the bread man, "My children do not steal!"

"They did!"

Pop stood tall over him and shouted, "Don't come here and say that again!"

After the bread man had left, muttering under his breath, my sweet-toothed brothers thought they had pulled one over on him. But they should have known that Pop would have the last word, since he had control over most everything we did.

After the dust had settled, my brothers sat in a circle on the other side of the hedge as Gus doled out the doughnuts without a care in the world. The mischievous, hungry thieves were intent on gobbling down this unexpected treat from heaven. Suddenly, Pop appeared out of nowhere and cracked Gus over the head with a hard knuckle. He turned and kicked the others all the way back to the house. Once there, they knew the drill, and lined up.

Pop's ominous face turned several shades of purple when he was angry, but that day he outdid even himself. His mug was a rainbow of rage. Nothing stood between us and the strict punishment he meted out at such times. The boys endured his outbursts. No one told on the other when someone got caught, at least hardly ever. Pop's knocks were one thing. But nobody wanted to suffer the terrible disgrace or the humiliation of being labelled a "snitch" or a "tattletale."

Whistleblowers they were not. I think Pop respected this trait in them, even when he disapproved of their behaviour. "Honour among thieves" was still honour of a sort, I suppose, and honour was highly prized by our father.

However, this did not save them. Pop bailed the boys out of trouble when he felt they were in the right, but if they were in the wrong, they had to duck for cover!

You would think that after this incident the boys would be more cautious whenever the Canada Bread truck arrived, but you'd be wrong. The pull of the delicious doughnuts was simply too strong. The next time the doors were left open for a crime of opportunity, they recruited Vince to be the lookout while they hid the doughnuts deep in the woods, much farther from the house where Pop was not apt to look for them. They hated the beatings, but they loved the doughnuts more. Even our father's swift justice could never stop them from stealing such a rare and wonderful treat.

Thanks for Your Support

My oldest sister Caroline led the way as we crossed the dark-stained floor of the one-storey Woolworth's department store in early June 1955, just before my fourteenth birthday.

"Come on, Peanut, hurry up! Stop dragging your feet."

I wish she'd stop calling me Peanut, I thought. *What a stupid nickname.*

"I don't need one and I don't want one. Let's just go home, Caroline."

She grabbed my hand and pulled me along. "Stop arguing about it. It's time for you to start wearing a bra." Caroline clenched my hand even tighter and marched me up to the counter.

A saleslady looked over her rhinestone studded cat's eyeglasses as she separated and folded undergarments at the counter. She removed her glasses with one hand and stood up straight with her shoulders back, emphasizing her robust chest under the tight-fitting pink cashmere sweater she wore. I swear she could not even see her feet over that heap. Her specs swung from a gold chain around her neck and and dangled off her chest, the chain matching her gold-capped front tooth.

I had managed to avoid this day for some time, and now almost fourteen, it seemed like boobs were everywhere.

"Excuse me," Caroline said. "My kid sister needs a bra; it's her first one. I don't know the size, maybe 32A. You'll need to measure her."

32A? She must be crazy!

"That's a horse size," I said. "I won't wear that. I just won't!"

"I'll pick out a few different sizes and styles for her to try on," the saleslady said, ignoring me completely. "Girls her age usually start with a soft cup bra rather than padded, maybe size 30A. I call them undergraduate bras." She laughed.

Caroline broke into muffled giggles at the phrase and the sales-lady, as if closing a sale, laughed even harder.

"Never heard them called that before," Caroline said, now braying with laughter.

Could she possibly be any louder? I thought, glaring at the two of them. *Why don't you announce it over the intercom?*

Everyone around us could surely hear them. My face flushed red. I gave the woman the dirtiest look I could muster and wanted to say, "What about your pointy, super-deluxe, 44-double D bra— they remind me of the headlights on a '55 Caddy."

In silence, I slithered along the counter, away from the two hyenas and pretended to look at the sleepwear while the great debate continued on the pros and cons of the Vogue undergradu-ate bra versus the padded bra versus the Playtex bra.

"Peanut, come over here," my sister yelled loud enough for them to hear her in Mexico. "What are you doing way over there? Come here and don't be silly."

Caroline pushed a white cotton bra against my chest, stretch-ing and flexing the band, coarsely measuring band size without being sensitive to my shyness. She fingered the bra and measured with her hand while checking the elastic, pulling the cups, and holding it up by the straps.

"Can't we just take it home and I'll try it on there?" I pleaded.

"We have to make sure it fits, silly."

She looked at my sullen expression.

"Look, Peanut. You're fourteen and people can see your boobies popping out of your sweater."

She was right. I could no longer ignore the fact that it had become necessary to wear a bra.

"Caroline," I exclaimed, my face growing even redder than before. I grabbed the bra from her and stormed toward the dressing rooms. She followed me in.

"Try it on," she said. She stepped back outside the curtain and pulled it closed.

I fumbled around but couldn't figure how to fasten the bra.

"Are you okay in there?"

"Yes," I yelled.

Caroline came back in and hooked it for me, adjusting and tugging and pulling it into place like I was a baby. My recently-formed breasts finally fell into place and filled the cups. Caroline stood back and looked at me, assessing the fit, tugging me this way and tugging me that way. The saleslady popped in.

"Everything okay in here?"

"No," I said, showing I was annoyed by slinging the rigged contraption over the doorframe. I was feeling used and abused. "I'll take it. Let's go home."

"That will be $1.79," she said. Then she looked closer and found an insignificant brown stain on the bra. "Make it $1.50."

New and stiff, this 34B Vogue bra completely bound and constricted my movement. Not only was it uncomfortable, but it was ugly! The stitching spiralled around the pointy cup resembled a hornet's nest. I sulked all the way back to the farm. My mood darkened with each mile, knowing all the teasing that awaited me.

I ran upstairs when we got to the house, before anyone could confront me. I looked in the mirror. Examining the outline of my body from the right side, and then from the left side, I pushed and poked the protruding objects side to side with outstretched fingers, inhaling and exhaling, watching the rise and fall of my bosom. I felt completely detached from them. I raised them, then lowered them. I pushed them down, trying to flatten them.

It was hopeless. My breasts were here to stay.

I joined my family in the living room. I felt my boobies arrive in the living room two steps ahead of me.

"Let's see how you look," my father said in front of all the boys. He stood up, turned me by the shoulders, and took a step backwards. I slumped forward, red-faced, my downcast eyes anxious and furtive. Without thinking, I crossed my arms over my chest. Pop unfolded my arms with tender care.

"That's better," he said. "Now all the bouncing will stop."

"But how can I go to school looking like this with these things in front of me? None of the other girls wear a bra. All the boys will know I'm wearing one!"

I didn't want to give any more ammunition to the boys at school who bullied and teased me all the time.

My brothers snickered.

"Marie's wearing beanies with chin straps," Nunzio laughed.

"She's wearing a slingshot," Mike teased.

"She's my *udder* sister," Louie squeaked. "Moo!"

Louie pulled the band in the back, snapping it hard. "She's got two buckets. She can carry water from the well in them," he teased.

The boys laughed and tossed slurs back and forth. I turned around and faced my jeering siblings. "Stop it," I cried. I turned to my father and said, "Make them stop it!"

"Okay, boys, stop it!" he yelled. "Quit teasing your sister."

The bra did give credibility to my new status of womanhood, but it didn't make me feel proud. It gave me a knotted feeling in the pit of my stomach. I felt tied down. If that pointy bra could have talked, it would have said, "Come too close and you might lose two eyes."

I thought I'd be treated more delicately at home. No longer would I be one of the boys climbing trees, running through the back bush and green fields, and playing baseball, football, hockey and Cowboys and Indians. Until then, my only companions were my eight brothers living at home. In fact, I had even looked like a boy, always wearing their hand-me-downs. Now everything was changing. I just wanted to go back to yesterday when things were normal. I didn't know how to cope, and so I retreated to my bed and cried myself to sleep.

The next morning my father shouted, "Nunzio, Mike, Marie! Hurry or you'll be late for the milk truck."

"I have a sore stomach!" I hollered and stayed under the covers. I pulled the itchy coat over my head, unable to rise above the millstone that humiliated me.

Soon after the boys left, my father's mammoth figure stood in the doorway of the closet where I slept.

A week earlier, Pop had moved me into my own room, just big enough for a single bed and a tiny dresser. Segregated from my brothers, I felt lonely and isolated. For the first time in my life, I shared a room with no one. Mice scratching in every corner of my new room mortified me. Creaking walls and loose tree branches slapping the window petrified me. Then, as the night grew longer, the sound of the silence magnified. I wanted the security and protection of my siblings, the even breathing of several kids in the room.

Pop entered my room, a spoon in one hand and a bottle of Castor Oil in the thick grizzly fingers of the other.

"You *must* be sick, Dolly," he said, "because I know how you hate to miss school."

Whenever tender moments passed between us, he always called me by the nickname he had given me, Dolly. Pop sat down on the edge of my bed and felt my forehead.

"Here, Dolly, take this for your sore stomach and stay in bed."

Great, I thought. I won't be forced to attend school. I felt a sense of relief settle over me.

"Tomorrow you'll feel better," he said. "You can go back to school then."

He stood up and looked down at me. He was being almost gentle.

"But you still have to wear the bra."

The Salvation Army Turkey

The events leading up to Christmas always held magic and wonderment for me and my multitude of brothers and sisters. The winter of 1955 was no different.

Every school morning, before venturing out into the unyielding deep freeze, we sat in a lineup on a bench by the back door and waited for my father to reach us one by one. Pop edged his way along the row, morning after morning, and wrapped each of our feet with newspaper and secured them with a piece of butcher string. After that was done, he fastened our thin rubber boots to our feet. Next, he put on our jackets, scarves and toques, then our mismatched mittens—or socks for mittens, which were old with holes in them.

After the Christmas pageant, which signalled the end of school for the year, we were free from the demands of waking up at five-thirty every morning and walking for what seemed like forever in the extreme weather to our one-room schoolhouse.

The General Store in Russell, about two miles down the road, stocked all sorts of tiny objects and goods for purchase. Pop gave us ten cents each to shop for Christmas gifts for one another at the General Store. He dictated for whom we should buy gifts. "Marie, you buy for Pat and Vince. Mike, you buy for Frank and Louie."

The Salvation Army Turkey

My brothers and I passed each other in the narrow aisles several times, scrutinizing the goods for sale on the wooden tables. Everything was in plain sight, so we held the merchandise close to our chests to prevent anyone attempting to peek at the purchase. I bought a pencil for Pat and an eraser for Vince for five cents apiece. As soon as we returned home, I wrapped my gifts for them in newspaper and tied them with white string. I wanted it to be a big surprise.

On Christmas Eve morning, we clamoured around the Salvation Army turkey that my father brought home. We jumped up and down with glee as Pop set the huge mound on the floor. The massive birds were donated to poor families like ours.

Pop stomped his boots and shook the snow from his long army coat with the shiny brass buttons that he kept pristine. "These coats never wear out," he once commented. He wore his army coat all his life and kept it in great shape.

"Let me see! Let me see! Stop pushing me!"

"Stop fighting!" he ordered. "You'll all get to see it!"

Pop picked up the heap, set it on the table, and slowly unfolded the butcher paper and string, finally revealing the massive turkey. The sight of the colossal bird always excited us. We immediately wanted to help clean out the monster. We closed ranks and prepared for the ensuing battle: who would be the first to stick their hand into the cavity of the turkey and pull out some smelly old guts? We pulled out all the pinfeathers and everything from inside the turkey. We loved the squishy feel and suction sound as we fought and tugged and pulled out the innards. Gleeful "oohs" and "yuks" ricocheted throughout the room. It was disgusting! It was delightful! It was Christmas! We really clobbered that turkey.

Noreen made delicious homemade stuffing. After jamming the stuffing into the bird, twelve little hands helped carry the pan as we edged our way to the stove and wedged the bird into the oven. We grunted as we pushed and squeezed it in. The bird was so big it touched all sides of the woodstove. Not only did the woodstove oven work overtime all night to cook the thirty-pound bird for our consumption on Christmas Day, but it also warmed the house and filled the air with wonderful smells.

My father kept vigil over the turkey, basting it as needed, and each time he opened the oven door that terrific aroma wafted out and sent us reeling as we inhaled and savoured the heady scent. We squabbled over the basting of the turkey—pushing, elbowing and jabbing our way to the front of the oven was a contest. The strongest among us got the best view.

As the turkey roasted, we washed our old and threadbare socks, the very socks we wore every day and, one by one, handed them to my father. Pop then nailed them in a neat line to the wooden slats where the wall was missing huge chunks of plaster. He held the nails in his mouth and tapped them in one at a time, tap, tap, tap, as each of us watched and fidgeted, waiting our turn to hand him our sock.

"Do mine next!" we yelled. "Do mine next!"

They didn't look like much, drooping lifelessly on the nails. Still, they were blessed with our anticipation, waiting for the hand of a white-bearded special someone to fill them with the treats we had looked forward to all year long: mint or cinnamon-flavoured hard Christmas candies, which we always traded back and forth for the ones we especially liked, a handful of nuts, one orange, and several lumps of coal.

"If you're bad, Santa will put a piece of coal in your stocking," Pop warned us each year. We usually got two or three chunks of coal apiece. If ever we received the full force of our father's wrath in any given year, we were sure to receive four or five lumps of coal.

The Salvation Army Turkey

We didn't realize until we were older that the coal wasn't for bad behaviour. Instead, the pieces of coal prevented the candies and nuts from falling through the holes in our socks.

Excitement levels mounted and by Christmas Eve we could hardly stand it. Some of us had figured out why Santa never revealed himself and why we could never catch him in the act—"Santa" was our older brothers and sisters who now lived in the city. But, no matter how hard we tried to stay awake and catch them in the act, we were nestled alongside each other in deep sleep long before they arrived home.

By early Christmas morning, the fire in the stove had died out and my father fuelled it again with dry wood that Gus and Lou had split in the covered shed the day before. Along with the turkey and stuffing and all the trimmings, we always added pasta and meatballs to our feast. Waking up Christmas morning to the aroma of the slow-cooked turkey and the whiff of sauce laced with garlic and onions was heaven.

At first light of dawn, we raced down the stairs to see if Santa had revealed himself and to see the magic that had occurred during the night. Miraculously, stockings had been filled with candies, oranges, nuts and, yes, coal. We inhaled the fragrance of the freshly-cut pine tree, strong and pungent, and marvelled at the strung popcorn and paper decorations.

At that time there were sixteen kids living at home, and we each received six gifts wrapped separately, for a total of ninety-six gifts under the tree that reached three feet high!

In one wrapped gift, we got socks. In another, we got underwear. The other gifts were mittens, hats, pyjamas and a simple toy from our father, all wrapped in plain, unadorned paper without decorations.

Hymns and Christmas carols played on the radio all day long.

On this particular Christmas Day, we didn't attend church as we usually did. The snow, ice and howling winds prevented the trip. It was probably just as well; my father couldn't handle the excitement and anxiety of his sixteen wound-up children. In church, you could always hear his impatient, exasperated voice as he ordered under his breath, "Nunzio, stop talking! Mike, take that gum out of your mouth! Louie, sit up straight!"

I was surrounded by brothers all the time which didn't lend anything to my femininity. I wore their hand-me-down coveralls and jeans, their plaid flannel shirts, their shoes, boots, coats and everything else for that matter.

That Christmas, the Christmas of my fourteenth year, was special. For the first time in my life, I got a brand new dress from my father and a little black lacquered jewellery box from my brother Nunzio, who by then had a job. When I opened the jewellery box, a ballerina pirouetted and twirled to tinkling music. Tiny, multi-faceted mirrors lined the box and made it look as if there were twelve ballerinas dancing that sparkled in the prisms.

The new second hand dress Pop gave me was a stunning turquoise taffeta that had a rhinestone buckle pinned to the drop-waist. The dress rustled when I walked. I didn't care that I had no place to wear it except on Christmas Day. I felt like a princess in the dress as I spun around in a circle and whirled around the room. I didn't sit down the whole day for fear of getting it wrinkled. It was the loveliest dress I had ever seen.

My father *had* told me that one day I would own a pretty dress and his prediction had come true.

My older sisters gave me a brand new winter coat; it was my first belted winter-weight long coat. The glorious rusty colour didn't match a thing I had, but I prized it. I wore the coat throughout the day and couldn't stop petting it.

The Salvation Army Turkey

When we finally sat down to turkey dinner, my father said, "Marie, take off that coat!" I didn't want to but, of course, I did.

I can't remember what anyone else got that year because I was too busy crying all day from happiness.

Creating Thuggery

Nunzio trudged home one afternoon with a heavy burden on his soul. Or rather in his pocket. A letter. Addressed to our father. From a teacher. The heaviest letter he ever carried.

Mrs. Powter, a rather dour science teacher, was the letter writer, and she had bad news for Pop—news we didn't want him to hear. But, of course, the letter and its contents would be known to our father as soon as he returned home from work.

Her instructions had been clear. "Give this to your father," she had told Nunzio, her eyes glaring, "the minute he gets home!"

The walk home from school that day was the longest of our lives.

The dreaded missive lay on the kitchen table for several hours as we waited for our father. Nunzio, Mike and I paced back and forth from the table to the window, from the window to the table, practically wearing a path in the floorboards, peeking through the window anxiously as we waited for the headlights to turn into the lane leading up to our house. If a watched pot never boils, I figured, watching the road might mean a similar delay in our father's return. A nice thought. But none of us held out much hope for any such reprieve.

Louie picked up the envelope for the third time, once again reading aloud the name of the addressee. "*Mr. Marini.* Yup, that's Pop alright," he exclaimed unnecessarily, even more excited than the previous two times. He was practically frothing at the mouth. "Boy, you guys are gonna get it."

Before any of the condemned could manage a reply, Mike spotted headlights turning into our long, bumpy driveway. The old DeSoto bounced up and down like a rubber ball, its shocks long since shot and never replaced.

"He's home," Mike shouted, again unnecessarily. We saw our executioner arrive mere seconds after Mike had, and we scattered to our bedrooms.

Nunzio hid in the upstairs closet.

I heard my father's heavy, deliberate footsteps coming up the stairs with ominous purpose. Fathers seem to carry themselves differently when they're angry, and ours was no exception. He seemed to move more heavily when he was mad at us, as if he was making his way across the surface of the moon—which was exactly where I wished I was when I heard the bedroom door open.

Shutting my eyes tight, I lay on my stomach under my bed in a dark corner of the room trying to make myself invisible. I even held my breath, as if exhaling might serve as a precursor to some type of child global positioning device.

"Come out from under there," Pop said, without even looking for me.

How did he always know?

I waited, just in case.

A broomstick poked me in the leg.

"I said come out of there."

"No," I pouted. "You'll hit me."

"You're darn right I will," he threatened.

I didn't move. I could almost hear his jaw tighten.

"You come out from under there right now, or you're going to get it even worse!"

Not for the first time that day, I began to cry.

The whole thing had started months earlier. On my first day in grade nine, Jean-Guy and David and Barry, the three worst bullies in the school, had immediately pegged me as quiet and submissive, which meant I was bully-bait, an easy target.

This school was very different from the tiny one-room schoolhouse in Marvelville that housed a total of twenty-three students, half of whom were my own brothers. The three-storey brick structure in Russell had more than two hundred students. I was seriously outnumbered. I was used to my brothers picking on me, sure. But they were my brothers. That was practically their after-school job. But the guys at my school were relentless. They made me completely miserable and I could not avoid their prejudice.

As a matter of fact, my only real friend at the school was Diane, who was also an outcast. She endured daily taunting about her pimply face and chunky two-hundred-pound body. Aching for friendship and yearning for inclusion, we were quite the pair of what the kids today would call "losers."

What we really were, of course, was lonely.

I remember standing on the school steps each morning, frantically searching out Diane, so we could walk to class together in case we encountered any of the Neanderthals. I panicked when groups of students came toward me when I stood alone, fearing a sneak attack. The three stooges would even chase me across the football field if they spotted me at lunchtime. Ironically, I would venture away from the school as far as possible while still remaining on school grounds, which only served to isolate me even more.

Had I stayed among the larger groups, I might have blended in a bit better and escaped the bullies' wrath.

Sometimes Jean-Guy and his fellow classmates cornered me at the school's back wall and smothered me with all sorts of derogatory questions. They pulled my hair and yelled, "Hey, Wop" or "Blackie" or "Hey, Eyetie, how many kids in your family, thirty-seven or thirty-eight?"

They once threw me to the ground and stood on my book bag. "Why are you here? Nobody even likes you! Why don't you go back to where you came from?" they shouted, as if I'd come from another planet. They threw the book bag at me and hit my head. Most days I ate my lunch in one of the stalls in the girls' washroom, for fear they would seek me out and run me down. There were many times when they ran up behind me unexpectedly and punched me in the middle of my back, taking my breath away.

At that age, nothing is more important to a child than fitting in. Their comments cruelly reinforced my naturally awkward feelings.

I looked up at them through feral, slit eyes, trying unsuccessfully not to cry. The thought had crossed my mind that perhaps they were jealous of my achievements as I had always scored one hundred percent on all my French and history tests. Their judging eyes shrank my accomplishments. I don't know if I've ever hated anyone more than I did them. They say you never again make friends like you do at that age. I suppose you don't make enemies like that, either.

"You don't belong here, Wop! You stink!"

I cried even harder, which only encouraged them.

"Tell your father to go back where he belongs!"

Each day was worse than the day before. I was miserable. I didn't sleep well, my appetite suffered, and my self-esteem—not all that strong to begin with—spiralled downward. I hated going to school; my love of learning left me. I walked around every day with a dark cloud hanging over my head. I held my breath whenever I walked by them, praying I would pass invisibly and unnoticed, hoping they would neither see nor hear me.

Nunzio and Mike were a grade ahead of me and their athletic abilities made them immune to harassment, in spite of the bullies' dislike of my family. Typical bullies are also cowards, and thus they prey on the weak. My brothers were never seen as weak. I thought they might help me, and I complained to them once, but I was too ashamed to give them the full picture. In my family, we fought like cats and dogs, but at the end of the day we were still family, and no whining was allowed.

"Jean-Guy and David and Barry pick on me all the time," I finally told my brothers. "They won't leave me alone."

"Just ignore them," Mike told me. "Nobody likes a cry-baby."

I was particularly dreading the usual torture on that fateful day when all the bullying finally came to a head. During our hike to school, I dragged my feet along the dirt road, hating my life. I asked myself, *Why do all of our schools always have to be two miles away?* Soon my brothers were far ahead of me, their long strides leaving me behind. Nunzio turned around when he realized I was not keeping up.

"Come on! We're going to be late because of you!"

Time and again my brothers stopped and waited, yelling at me to hurry up as I stood bawling. Finally, they both marched back grumbling to me.

"Here, give me your lunch," Mike said and shoved it in his jacket.

"Give me your books," Nunzio said and jammed them inside his jacket. "Now come on!"

Flanked by my two brothers, the three of us arm in arm, I was hauled the final mile to school, my feet barely touching the ground. We arrived in record time, even though there was snow on the ground. This only meant there would be even more time for the bullies to harass me. It was the winter of my misery.

I had been suffering their bullets and dodging their arrows for months, and I didn't know how much longer I could take it.

As it turned out, not for much longer.

Nunzio and Mike were of medium builds, but they were both farm boys, and much stronger than they looked. Nunzio, especially, had powerful arms and big, beefy hands that we called his bear claws. If he grabbed my shoulder a little too hard in play, it brought me to my knees. His hands were like our father's hands.

That first semester I was ranked the best table tennis player in the entire school, in spite of never having played the game before. Jean-Guy, who also played, didn't like being upstaged by a girl, let alone me. At lunchtime that day, he challenged me to a game.

Big mistake.

I loathed him so much by this time that I eagerly accepted the challenge, not thinking of the consequences when I beat him in front of all his friends. Which, of course, I did—11-0.

His friends teased him mercilessly.

"You got beat by a Wop! A *girl* Wop!"

I'm not sure which bothered him more, my heritage or my gender. I suppose it was probably my gender, but whatever, Jean-Guy took it badly.

All hell broke loose.

Furious and embarrassed, he lunged at me, yanking my long black hair. I was wearing a brand-new barrette my father had given me for Christmas the month before, his only gift to me save for a handful of candies and an orange. The barrette came off in his hand, along with a good bit of my hair, and I screamed in pain. Jean-Guy turned and threw the barrette out the third-floor window and it disappeared into the softly falling snow. I cried for the barrette far more than for the pain I was in.

That did it!

Finally unable to tolerate the fear in the pit of my stomach any longer or the bullying any further, I slammed down my paddle and went after him. At first, I shook and sobbed uncontrollably. I don't think I ever felt such overpowering fury, and the anger made me cry harder. There's something about losing it in front of others that is liberating in its intensity. All my inhibitions went out the window following the loss of my barrette. Endorphins kicked me into overdrive.

"You bastard!" I screamed, completely unconcerned that if my father had heard me say that word he'd beat me plenty. Jean-Guy's eyes went wide, and for an instant the entire room became quiet.

It was the calm before the storm.

I went for him, clawing and scratching, and he turned and ran away like, well, a girl. I chased him around the desks, in between the desks and over the desks, oblivious to all but my rage.

Jean-Guy must die.

The other kids screamed and cheered as we ran around the room and out the door, down the third-floor hallway, and then back to homeroom. He was tall and thin and very fast, and my short legs couldn't catch up to him. Every time I got close, he managed to slip from my grasp.

I grew angrier and more pumped.

The more he eluded me, the more frustrated I became. But I wouldn't stop. I couldn't. Blinded by rage and like an animal whose life depended on catching its prey, I became a volcano that had erupted. Fuelled by adrenaline, I hopped onto a desk and took flight just as Jean-Guy made the fatal mistake of attempting to take a short cut toward the door.

The eagle landed.

With talons out, I hit Jean-Guy with full force, tearing into the back of his pressed white shirt as he screamed and stumbled forward. The force of my attack nearly knocked him to the floor, but he managed to stay on his feet and pull away. However, the entire back of his shirt had ripped open in my claws—buttons flew, children gasped, and the rabbit screamed. Jean-Guy tried to run, but I had wounded my prey, and I knew with certainty that vengeance, long delayed, was finally mine.

I shoved him with all my might and knocked him to the floor. He rolled over and tried to fight me off. In a move that Hulk Hogan might later envy, I drove my knee into his chest and all the fight went out of him. I pounded his face like a wild thing until his nose bled all over his shredded white shirt. All my emotional injuries and pent-up rage flowed out. I couldn't stop. Nunzio and Mike, and one of Jean-Guy's friends, finally managed to pull me off him, but not before I mashed his face. I think they were more tired from their efforts than I was.

I stood up, heaving and sobbing, and they helped my mortal enemy to his feet. He looked like twelve miles of bad road with his clothes ripped to shreds and his face a bloody mess. He was thoroughly worn out and defeated. I knew then that he would think twice before picking on me again without an army to back him up.

Without a word said, Jean-Guy's friends helped him walk away, and I collapsed against Nunzio's chest. Through wrenching sobs, I told my brothers about how Jean-Guy and his friends had tormented me for months. Nunzio's eyes grew dark, his jaw tightened. His look again reminded me of our father's.

"We'll take care of it," he said.

Nunzio and Mike turned and strode from the room, their fists twisting and red. I ran behind them to see the avengers in action. They spotted Jean-Guy sitting on a bench outside, huddled with his friends. His back to my brothers, he didn't see Nunzio and Mike approach with clenched fists. I walked in front of the group to draw their attention. Jean-Guy looked up and sneered, still smug even after his beating. Just as he was about to say something, which I'm sure would have held all the snark he could muster, Nunzio tapped him on the shoulder.

"Leave my sister alone," he said, "or else."

Jean-Guy stood up and turned to face my brother with his friends around him.

"Or else *what?*"

I wish I could have seen the look on his face just before Nunzio's fist smashed into his already swollen nose, but I got to see it soon enough when Jean-Guy spun around. The blood splattered in drops, punctuating the snow. He tumbled to the ground, face first at my feet. Maybe he would find my barrette while he was down there.

As soon as he stood back up, Nunzio clobbered him again, and the familiar chant of "fight! fight!" echoed across the schoolyard. As the other children gathered around, Nunzio grabbed Jean-Guy by the collar and threw him down hard. Mike put his foot on Jean-Guy's throat.

"Don't ever hit my sister again."

Mike held up a clenched fist an inch from his face so that Jean-Guy would fully understand the benefits of having a large family of Italians at your back.

Our moment of triumph was, alas, all too short, as a familiar voice shouted across the yard. The crowd parted like the Red Sea and there stood the bully's own personal Moses, arriving just in time to deliver him from my brother, the Pharaoh.

Mrs. Powter grabbed Nunzio and Mike by their ears and hauled them to the office. She ordered me to follow and I chased behind them. It was the least I could do after their wonderful display of brotherly protection. She sat us down and began to write on a single sheet of paper. It didn't take long, but it seemed like an eternity. She folded the letter, placed it inside an envelope, and sealed it ominously. She stood up and handed it to my brother.

"Give this to your father as soon as he gets home."

All the way home we speculated about the contents of the letter. We had different feelings, different understandings, different perspectives. The letter was sealed, but of course we opened the envelope, and with our heads huddled together, we read it aloud.

> *Dear Mr. Marini,*
> *Your daughter Marie and your sons, Nunzio and*
> *Michael were sent to detention after school today*
> *for creating thuggery in the schoolyard.*
> *I would like to speak with you tomorrow*
> *regarding this matter.*
> *Sincerely,*
> *Mrs. Powter.*

We looked up in unison.

"Creating thuggery?" Mike said. "What the hell is that?"

"Thuggery," Nunzio said and repeated the word again with bewilderment. "It means excitement."

"Well, all the kids *were* cheering," Mike added hopefully.

"No, it's something bad," I said. "Otherwise, she wouldn't be writing to Pop."

"Let's look it up in a dictionary when we get home," Mike suggested.

"We don't have a dictionary, dummy," Nunzio answered.

"Well," Mike said, "I think it means we're all gonna get it."

We slid the letter back into the envelope and resealed it.

Unspoken between us was the option of not showing the letter to our father, which, though tempting, was a terrible idea. We had to give it to him. Mrs. Powter would never drop it, and when she spoke to Pop the next day, things would really be bad if he was surprised.

So, Pop would have to read the letter.

Nunzio set the letter on the table when we got home and the waiting began. At the end of the day, there were certain immutable facts. One of them was that our father never accepted any excuse for defying a teacher or anyone else in authority. Detention was nothing compared to the fate that awaited me as I slowly crawled out from under the bed to accept my punishment.

I won't go into all the gory details, but suffice to say it was as bad as I imagined it would be.

Still, I recall the events of that day fondly. It was quite a bonding experience with my brothers who, for some reason, never again picked on me quite as much—perhaps the memory of how I chased down my attacker lingered in their minds. And, somehow, that had made it all the worthwhile.

The next day when he met with Mrs. Powter, my father realized she had it in for us. He came home and said, "You all did the right thing. Don't ever let anyone treat you like that again."

By the end of the school year, I had reached a blazing moment of truth. I would never go back to that school.

Because You're a Girl

The summer I turned fifteen, my sisters Caroline and Josephine had taken me to the city, with my father's permission of course, to work with them as a "spotter" in a dry cleaning plant. The condition attached was that Nunzio and Mike were to bring me home every weekend in our 1947 DeSoto.

On any given Friday night, my sisters each took home a customer's dress they wanted to wear to the Saturday night dance, and returned the dresses on Monday morning, dry-cleaned and ready for customer pickup. Their friends thought they'd spent a lot of money on clothing, what with wearing a "new" dress to the dance every Saturday night.

A horrible heat wave hit Ottawa. I stood all day long for three weeks in unbearable temperatures, working with reeking, potent chemicals, removing spots from clothes, and steaming them with a hand steamer. The heat, the humidity, the steam and the chemicals gave me severe headaches and made me sick. Was this the life that awaited me?

The previous two summers away from the farm, I had worked with Josephine in a greasy spoon slinging hash, and so I was used to hard work. But that summer, although Josephine and Caroline were pivotal figures in my life, I resolved that I wanted better jobs than my siblings had, that I needed to enrich myself, that I wanted to live better than I did in my early years.

This only fueled the fire between my father and me in our battle over my education. That fire had become a blaze that threatened to consume us both.

I lowered my head and wept into my freshly-pressed blouse. "They hate me here! I want to go to school in the city!"

Hearing no response, I looked up at my unyielding father and beseeched him with my eyes.

"Please," I begged. "I'll behave, I'll study hard, and I'll do whatever you say!"

Pop raised an eyebrow at that last promise. Was I making progress? Was he softening? Had I gone too far?

"If I have to go to another year of high school here, I'll die," I cried dramatically.

Obviously skeptical of my impending demise, his eyebrow fell. At that moment I had my answer—I was going back to the country school.

When I was home, my weekend chores seemed especially onerous, what with all the ironing and prepping food, while the boys visited their friends on neighbouring farms for fun and games until the sun went down. Sure, they had their chores, but like all teenagers, my world revolved around my own problems and I wasn't going to let details like that intrude on my pity party.

Staring aimlessly at the rising steam, I pushed the iron back and forth across the dampened cloth, careful not to tarry at any single spot for long lest I scorch my brothers' church clothes and further anger my father. Once finished, I stood the iron on end and looked out the window, watching the boys play. It was so unfair! I felt bitter tears welling up and angrily folded the last of my brothers' Sunday best.

I took exception to the different standards for the boys and deeply resented my father's indifference to my needs. Growing up surrounded by brothers, I had to be tough, and I was, but when I was alone, all my emotions and hormones let loose. Ironically, this only fuelled my father's beliefs about the differences between boys and girls. That his opinion was based on a partial truth made me that much more angry. I felt I had to always be decisive and stand my ground in order have the tiniest chance of being taken seriously. That was my sentence for having been born a girl.

If only we didn't have so many kids, I thought, *my burden wouldn't be as heavy.*

I once remarked to my father that I couldn't understand why baby after baby was born each year; the entourage never shrank. One child left home, another entered the world. I caught a backhand for my remark and never dared to say it again.

The summer flew past and my father's decision stood firm. He was a hard man, as stubborn as I was insistent. He would not reconsider. The thought of returning to that school in a few short weeks, and seeing Jean-Guy again, filled me with dread. I so badly wanted to attend school in the city. The last time I saw him, Jean-Guy had balled his fist and hit me so hard square in the middle of my back that I literally couldn't breathe. The memory had pained me the entire summer. For a long time, I didn't tell anyone about this incident. More often than not, I cried myself to sleep at night or stayed awake for hours because of him.

I first heard the insult "Wop" hurled across the gravel schoolyard by Jean-Guy and his equally detestable friend, David, while walking with my friend, Doris. She helpfully explained to me that my brothers and I were the only ones at school whose names ended in a vowel.

I was not used to fighting with my father. For most of the time, I obeyed him without question. Yet on the subject of switching schools, I refused to give up. This only made him all the more determined that I should comply.

"You're a girl," was his "reason" with me. "It's not important for you to finish high school. You'll get married, have babies, and your husband will take care of you."

"I can take care of myself."

"You're too young to move away from your family. And even if I could afford school in the city, the boys would go before you would. They'll have families to support one day."

"I'll get a job and pay my own way."

"I said no, and that's final!"

I ran to my room and refused to come out. How could Pop not understand the stupidity of a tradition that was choking me? *Did he not see a part of me was dying?* I wrote in my diary. The pages in the secret journal were the only thing that kept me sane that summer; they were my salvation. Before blowing out the lantern, I acknowledged the day's events in my diary, because during the time I spent writing, I was free.

> *Why am I always at odds with him? Why must there always be conflict? It seems there is no point in fighting for first place; though I am the first one in the family who wants to complete high school, it is a question of position. Ranking tenth among the children and being female is not a good place to be.*

For Pop to pay for my education was unthinkable. I understood my family's finances. To pay for school, I needed to learn a marketable skill. But I couldn't learn a marketable skill if I stayed enrolled at the country school. It was a classic Catch-22, although I don't think that phrase had yet been coined. All I knew was I felt stifled and oppressed.

Upon completing grade eight or turning sixteen, whichever came first, my brothers and sisters before me had been sent to the city to find a room for rent, get a job, and send money back home to help support the rest of the family. Whenever one child moved out, they were replaced with a newborn, and so the unforgiving cycle continued. I resented my father for making babies when he couldn't provide for the ones he already had. I could not call him on this again because I had already broken the first rule of our family: respect must be shown to my father no matter the circumstance. We didn't dare contradict him. Even the siblings who were independent did not question him or talk back. I don't think I ever even saw one of us light up a cigarette in his presence. It just wasn't done.

At fifteen, my sense of responsibility and independence was well developed, but somehow those battles with my father that summer left me unravelled. I became increasingly unhappy and refused to speak. The arguments affected me physically. My body stooped and lost its bounce. I was a mess.

"Set the table and put out the food for supper!" Pop barked at me one night. "I'm tired of arguing with you. You're not leaving home. You will continue at the country school."

I ran to the kitchen, crying and muttering under my breath, "Who does he think he is, the Supreme Court?"

I stormed around the kitchen where some of the boys were already seated at the table waiting to eat dinner. As I set the silverware, the cutlery flew from my hands and clanked against the plates. The potato masher angrily whipped the spuds into submission. The serving fork stabbed the sausages which were slammed down on each of the sixteen plates. The bread was lobbed onto the table. My father was about to put a stop to my antics, but just then two boisterous brothers grabbed for the same piece of bread, and he was forced to end their skirmish, and my actions were forgotten.

Or perhaps I was finally wearing him down.

I couldn't wait to vent my anger in my diary after the supper dishes were finished. When I reached the top of the stairs, I saw the soft glow of the lantern in my bedroom, the light creeping onto the landing. Someone was in my room. I tiptoed to the door, which was slightly ajar, and peeked inside.

My father sat on my bed, my diary in his thick, callused hands. I should have been angry, but I watched him hold the book open with such a gentle reverence, I immediately felt guilty for all the angry, negative thoughts I'd written down within its pages. Perhaps if I had talked to him calmly or in a more logical manner, Pop would have listened. Then I noticed something extraordinary. As he read, the lines in his forehead disappeared and his breathing evened out. Instead of anger, I sensed sadness. At that moment, I realized we had both missed the mark. I did not confront him. Instead, I slipped back downstairs and joined my siblings.

Sometimes when we least expect it, the world presents us with something we've never before encountered, something which teaches us a lesson about our humanity. I knew my approach with my father had been wrong; I needed a fresh strategy.

But how could I explain to Pop what I felt? He was reading all my angry thoughts and feelings, but I held deeper emotions for which I had no words. My inner yearnings were something that even I didn't fully understand. I just knew that I wanted more out of life than what had been planned for me.

I had seen things that made me aware of the poverty in which I lived—distinctive interiors with paintings and art objects displayed in unique ways, gleaming hardwood floors, real china instead of chipped enamel plates, rooms illuminated with electric lights and not dimly-lit lanterns, fresh clean bed linens rather than heavy winter coats, that were supposed to pass for blankets, over a mattress on the floor, pretty window treatments instead of unfinished fabric covering cracked windows. These things captivated me, yet I had only seen them in the home of Mrs. Fader, my one-room schoolhouse teacher.

Mrs. Fader's daughter, Alice, and I had become fast friends within the first few weeks of me attending Marvelville. She had invited me over for sleepovers once or twice a year and I couldn't stop touching and admiring all of their nice furnishings. I wanted my world to be like other people's, with carpeted floors and green plants and all manner of things attractively created. But where was it and how could I get there?

The next evening, my father interrupted my thoughts still churning from the night before.

"Marie, front and centre!"

I walked into the front room and stood before my father. He began to speak, but I quickly lost interest in his words, and began scrutinizing the curled flypaper hanging from the ceiling with hundreds of flies stuck to it, many struggling to free themselves. I began to cry. My desperation to free myself was no different than those poor insects.

"Did you hear what I said?"

I looked at my father. There was confusion on his face.

"I said you can move to the city. But you'll have to get a job. I can't support you."

I couldn't believe my ears, especially after he had read my diary. After so many months arguing with him, it seemed the dice had rolled in my favour. I threw my arms around his neck and cried even harder.

"You won't be disappointed," I told him. "I promise!"

"No boys, no dating, no fooling around; only study and hard work—and good grades!"

I couldn't speak. I just nodded and ran out of the room. I didn't stop running until I was cartwheeling outside under the full moon. I felt incredible—liberated. The feeling was indescribable. Suddenly, I could imagine a future beyond my world on the farm. The air smelled fresh and clean, and the stars twinkled more brightly than I'd ever seen them. As I stood on the spot where a few days earlier I had written in the dirt "I hate him," I was amazed to realize that my father had read my angry words and yet understood my deeper emotions. By the time I left home, the number of children had reached seventeen. Three of my brothers and sisters, Tony, Phyllis and Jimmy, were all under the age of six. I never had the chance to grow up with them.

And so, at the end of August 1956, freed at last from my father's grip, and never having accepted the words, "You can't do that because you're a girl," I packed my meagre belongings and moved from the sheltered confines of the farm to the City of Ottawa.

My life would never be the same.

Bright Lights, Big City

Spittle flew in my face as Mr. Scaff explained the rules of my employment. The gaunt owner of Scaff's Restaurant wore a white bib apron that hung from his veined neck and tied around his skinny waist. His salt and pepper hair, swept back with a generous amount of Brylcreem, showed white scalp. Sagging skin at the corners of his black eyes emphasized the dark bags underneath, and his wide, flat teeth protruded as he spoke.

"I pay thirty-five cents an hour," Mr. Scaff said in his thick Lebanese accent.

I nodded even though I knew that fifty cents an hour was the going rate.

"You'll work nine hours a day, seven days a week, from five p.m. to two a.m., except on Sundays, when you'll work nine a.m. to six p.m."

I nodded again. I was grateful for the work. I had no negotiating skills. He owned me.

I registered for school that same day.

Mary, my sister-in-law, had contracted tuberculosis. She was placed in a sanatorium for treatment. I stayed with her husband, my brother Steve, and his in-laws. They were very kind and gentle and so good to me. I felt protected and safe having a big brother in the same house with me.

Exactly one year later, Mary had recovered enough to return home. I moved to a little rented room with my sister, Jo. The room, in the rear of a three-room tumbledown on Kent Street, was so slanted you could roller skate down the sloping floors. Jo and I shared a double bed.

When at work, I kept my books open and pencil ready in the back booth of the restaurant, and for a few minutes here and there, I crammed in a little homework or worked on a simple budget for my shaky finances.

Whenever he noticed me jotting down homework, "Scab," as we had nicknamed Mr. Scaff, ordered me to wash down the booths or fill the sugar and ketchup bottles or the salt-and-pepper shakers or help empty the dishwasher in the kitchen or mop the floor or peel potatoes—anything to prevent me from sitting down and doing homework. He repeatedly barked in my face, never failing to shower me with spittle.

"I no pay you to look at zee books," he'd say.

Most nights after the sleazy Quality Hotel across the street ran all the drunks and bums out at midnight, they would come in and eat at Scaff's. One night, while I was taking their orders, one of them casually reached out and grabbed my breast. I couldn't believe it!

"How dare you!" I pushed him away. "Get your filthy hands off me!"

He grabbed me again. This time, I picked up a ketchup bottle and clobbered him over the head. I couldn't tell where the blood started and the ketchup ended. His buddies laughed. Another night, when a drunken hand wandered under my skirt, I spun around and poured a steaming pot of coffee into the offender's lap and was sworn at in a language I didn't recognize. The others laughed again.

"Such a big spirit in such a little girl," one of them said. "Come here, honey," he said, groping for me. I slapped his face.

"You can't treat customers like that!" Mr. Scaff screamed. "You're crazy! Get the hell out of here. You're fired!"

"Good," I said. "I hate this filthy place, I hate the grubby customers, and I hate you!"

Tired and overworked, I slammed down my pencil and pad, tore off my apron, and stomped out the door. But I returned after Mr. Scaff "allowed" me another chance.

Each time the men groped me, I retaliated. Each time I retaliated, Scab fired me on the spot. But, after a day or so, he would call me back to work. The termination of my employment allowed me a day or two of respite and made me feel better fortified to handle the next assault.

One night after the hotel closed, the same group of sleazy men marched into the restaurant. Mr. Scaff whispered to me as the gang came in, "Just let them touch you a little bit. They don't mean anything. They're drunk. Keep them happy." And then he winked, which made it even worse. I stormed out.

I returned two days later, of course, when he called me back once again.

Whenever a drunk tried to give him the slip without paying, Scab ran from behind the cash register brandishing a machete that he kept hidden behind the counter.

"You pay zee bill, or I'm gonna cut you down!" he screamed.

He usually got his money.

When my shift ended, I took a cab home at two in the morning and devoted two hours to homework, and then fell into bed at four, only to get up at eight for the walk to school. Every night,

I missed my family. I missed my younger brothers and the sound of their rhythmic breathing that had lulled me to sleep at night. I was acutely aware that I was alone.

After school, I walked to work. Time and finances did not permit me to stay behind with the other girls and have a ten-cent coke or fries after school. My youth, and my conviction, allowed me to carry out a crippling schedule, working sixty-three hours a week and attending school full time. I was always in a rush. I needed to save money for second hand winter boots, warmer socks, a heavier coat—there was always something. I managed to eke out a threadbare existence.

I had a horrific nightmare one night and cried on and off for most of the following day at school. A teacher asked me to stay back when the bell rang.

"Why are you crying?" she asked.

"My brother, Lou, is going to die of lung cancer," I told her.

"Is he sick in the hospital?"

I then told her that I had this nightmare the previous night and saw Louie dying in a hospital bed of lung cancer. A bright light and some family members had surrounded his bed. The teacher told me not to worry, that it had just been a bad dream. I dried my eyes and moved on to the next class.

More than two years later, I got sick and tired of the drunks and lowlifes at Scaff's and started looking for another job. Ultimately, I managed three part-time jobs: typing invoices in a men's clothing store 3:30 to 5:30 p.m., waiting tables at Scaff's 5:45 to 7:15 p.m., and from 7:30 p.m. onward caring for an eighty-eight-year-old invalid until her seventy-five-year-old spouse came home at midnight from his job as a commissioner at the local TV station. Despite this, the money barely carried me through. I felt that if I sat down I might not ever get back up again. The only way to keep going was to keep going.

I calculated my budget often, almost obsessively, as if doing so enough times would eventually change the end result: $15 a week for rent, $3 for transportation, and the balance of $4.05 for books, clothing and food.

When I left the farm for work and school, I hadn't realized that I was trading in one struggle for another. I knew it was going to be difficult, but I hadn't understood the enormity of such a workload—running from job to job, squeezing in homework, staying up all hours of the night to complete assignments, living on four hours of sleep, and running myself ragged. Fortunately, my teachers were understanding and didn't reprimand me when I took a day off each month to catch up on sleep.

Like my older siblings before me, I was expected to send some of my hard-earned money home to help support my younger siblings, but my earnings barely kept me going. It wasn't until a few years later that I was able to start sending money to Pop.

By age eighteen, I had a taste for the luxurious on a budget for a pauper. My finances demanded discipline. I knew things would improve if I kept at it. The desire for something better for myself drove me. I wanted knowledge, I wanted decent clothing, I wanted to travel, I wanted self-development. I wanted nice things—and I was going to get them no matter what! Having known true poverty, my dreams were of the good days to come, with a better job and more money in my pocket.

Once a month, on Friday afternoon, Nunzio and Mike arrived in front of the school in our old DeSoto and took me home for the weekend. It was wonderful to wake up the next morning at home. An explosion of tomato sauce laced with garlic and accented with basil tickled my nose at supper. When I ate, I knew I was home.

My father declared that I had lost weight, and on each visit he insisted on feeding me until I nearly burst. He literally pushed me into a chair and threw a plate of pasta in front of me.

"Mangia, mangia!" Pop said. "Eat, eat!"

My demanding schedule took its toll on me. For three years, I had no social life, no connection with my fellow students, no companionship, no meaningful friendships. In the city, I felt lonely and isolated. After putting up with all our fights and their special treatment, I missed my brothers.

When Josephine first moved to the city, she lived with Caroline in a rooming house and shared a room with a double bed and a single hotplate for cooking. Louie and Gus rented a room in the same house and lived in much the same conditions. Steve lived with his family and his in-laws. Everyone scraped by, thanks to menial jobs, but I missed the experience of living in close quarters, I missed the friendship, and I missed the conversation flying around the dinner table.

Most nights in the city, I curled up in bed and fell asleep in a state of exhaustion.

My Night with the King

I was usually a conscientious student, but on April 3, 1957, I could not concentrate. I fell into a steady daydream. English, arithmetic, history—no subject could possibly hold a candle to the anticipation that made my whole body quiver from the moment I got out of bed after having lain awake the entire night. My fifteen-year-old cousin Marie and I were about to experience a-once-in-a-lifetime event; a happening so amazing that we both could have happily died and gone to heaven, except we actually had tickets to heaven.

We had front row seats for the Elvis Presley performance at the Ottawa Auditorium.

The concert caused quite a stir in the city. Parents and teachers alike warned all teenagers against attending. They deemed Elvis's music as that of "the devil," but if this was true, then we were all possessed. As far as I was concerned, Elvis was a saviour who would rescue me from my awkward and troubled teenage years.

I pictured his eyes finding mine, boring deep into my soul. He would stop singing, hush the musicians, and quiet the hall.

As the entire audience held its collective breath, Elvis would walk to the edge of the stage, extend his hand, and as he helped me up onto the stage in front of the shocked hall, the King of Rock 'n' Roll would lean in close and gently whisper in my ear—

"Stay away," the principal's deep, emphatic voice boomed over the intercom, snapping me out of my daydream. "You are absolutely forbidden to attend the Elvis Presley concert. Any student found to be in attendance will be suspended."

Marie and I arrived at the auditorium three hours early, eagerly clutching our tickets. Hundreds of girls were already in line, chanting and shrieking. Feeding off each other, we whipped ourselves into a frenzied state.

"We want Elvis! We want Elvis!"

Pandemonium on the street forced the attendants to open the doors and let us in early. A barricade had been erected about twenty feet from the stage and police officers were posted every six feet to prevent the mob from getting close to Elvis. A half-hour before the concert, the MC teased and revved up the already uproarious crowd.

"Are you ready for Elvis?" he bellowed into the microphone.

We screamed in the affirmative. Our squeals seemed loud enough to pop eardrums and break the sound barrier. Then the uproar began in earnest.

"Do you love Elvis?" he hollered.

We did! Our out-of-control screaming seemed to cause even the overhead lights to shake.

"We want Elvis! We want Elvis!" thousands of fans chanted. As we screamed, the police tightened their queue and waved to reinforcements, who came running out of nowhere onto the floor, linking arms against our expanding waves.

Screaming teenage girls flouted the law—and limb—as they tried to throw their legs over the barrier.

Finally, the lights dimmed, save for a single spotlight on the stage, and he appeared. Wearing a gold jacket, black shirt, black pants and a gold medallion as big as my fist, Elvis walked onstage in white suede shoes and a jet black pompadour and sideburns. He walked out with a surprisingly simple gait, his guitar slung over one shoulder, one hand raised in greeting, and our hysteria went into overdrive. Emotions exploded. Elvis was awesome!

The fans roared, the lights shook, the roof raised, and the barricade advanced a few feet forward. We cheered, we screamed, we cried. Even more cops ran out in a mostly futile effort to push back the crowd.

Elvis put his hands to his ears as he looked out into the dark sea of high-pitched screaming faces and grinned with that sexy curled-up lip of his. Girls wept. As Elvis oozed sex onto nine thousand hyper teenage girls, some fainted and the police carried them out. Other fans quickly filled their empty spots as if they'd never been there.

For two and a half hours, with a half-sneer on his face and his hips grinding, Elvis sang and danced us into hysteria. Every movement was a new revelation. He rose up on the balls of his feet and back down, raised his arms, crooked his pinky finger, jerked his body this way and that way, and most of all, gyrated his hips in ways I had never imagined! Even today, when I remember his incredible charisma, I still get chills up and down my spine. Everything he did excited the unrestrained mob.

"Elvis, we love you!" I screamed.

"Elvis, Elvis, over here!" screamed others.

"Love Me Tender," "Teddy Bear," "Heartbreak Hotel," "Blue Suede Shoes," "Hound Dog" and many more songs blasted forth from his lips. We all knew the lyrics by heart. Like every other girl there, I felt that he was singing only to me!

The roar of the crowd never died down.

On TV, his moves had been restricted; the camera always showed him only from the waist up because the authorities had claimed, "Elvis is corrupting teenagers with his grinding hips." But at this concert, we saw it all, and it was the greatest night of my young life.

I was voiceless for three days afterwards.

A picture of me, stageside at the concert, appeared on the front page of the *Ottawa Citizen.*

At school the next day, the principal announced, "It has been reported that several students attended the Elvis Presley concert. If you are one of those students, please report to the office. Eventually, we will discover who you are."

Numerous students from various high schools across the city were suspended, including students from my school, but in spite of my photo on the front page of the *Ottawa Citizen,* screaming my head off, I somehow slipped by. I was either incredibly lucky or my teachers were no brighter than a Bundt cake.

Word spread throughout the school that I had close-up pictures of Elvis, and instantly I became someone to be envied.

But my father was no Bundt cake.

Two days after the concert, my older sister Jo wagged her finger and said, "Pop saw your picture in the paper. You're gonna get it."

Pop summoned me home. Nunzio and Mike drove into the city and picked me up. I rode the thirty-eight miles home, hemmed in by my brothers in the front seat, dreading every second. The conversation I expected to have with my father played out over and over in my head. What would my punishment be? What would he do to me? He always meted out military punishment. My heart quickened.

"What the hell did you think you were doing? You acted like a fool. You shamed yourself and you shamed me. Now everyone will only talk about how wild you are."

"But Pop, Marie and I just went to a concert, that's all. I swear I did nothing wrong. And I don't care what my aunts and uncles think."

"I should never have let you move to the city. You've run wild. Pack your things tomorrow and get back to the farm. No more school in the city for you."

It went almost exactly like that.

I clutched my hands together in a plea of forgiveness. My heart plunged. The waterworks began.

"Please Pop, give me another chance. I promise I won't do anything to embarrass you ever again! Please!"

My brothers and sisters looked on. I was the trailblazer in the family, and this was a big one. We all knew that if I was able to receive clemency, there would be hope for all of us.

He looked at me sternly.

"One more chance. You go to school, you go to work, and you study hard. No boys, no concerts, and no more wild behaviour!"

"Yes, Pop. I mean no, Pop."

"If I *ever* hear you've done anything like this again, your brothers will come get you and bring you right back home to stay."

My heaving body embraced him. Then I ran out of the room before he could change his mind. I had dodged a bullet!

Marie and I continued to see concerts during my high school years. We saw Buddy Holly and the Crickets, The Everley Brothers,

Patsy Cline, Ritchie Valens, The Big Bopper, Roy Orbison, Fats Domino, Little Richard, Johnny Cash and many others. It was the beginning of a cultural revolution, or as many racist critics of the time said, "The influence of rhythm and blues and gospel-related music is a Black conspiracy!"

But Elvis prevailed. Today the King is credited with melding rhythm and blues with country music in a way no one had before. It was the birth of Rock 'n' Roll, a huge breakthrough for the times. I was there. I was part of it. And I will never forget it. The experience of being mere feet away from the King of Rock 'n' Roll left me "all shook up." He made the music we loved. He dared to rock. Before Elvis, there was nothing.

And on that night, only thirty-seven of the two hundred and fifty-nine Members of Parliament showed up for a night session in the House of Commons.

The rest were at the concert.

Fifteen-year-old Marie Margis on the right, her cousin Marie on the left.

A Big Lesson Learned

As graduation drew near, I knew I could not keep up the demanding pace of full-time work and attending school. I resented the fact that I did not have sufficient funds to continue schooling. It was disheartening. What a blow. I loved school and learning so much and hated the prospect of not returning. So I made a decision. The same day school ended, I pulled myself together, gathered my things, and left for Toronto.

Meek and quiet before, now I was strong and outspoken. I was no longer shy nor ashamed of my background, but outgoing and proud. When I left the farm, I had been raw and naive. Now, I was polished and experienced. After having entered the big city as a blank slate, I was now closer to the person I had always wanted to be.

I was in Toronto for only a week when I found a job. The Ottawa school had awarded me top honours in office skills, and I found a good-paying typing job working for stockbrokers. I felt that I had found my niche.

During my first year of full-time work, I completed my matriculation through night school, and started to live a little. Work afforded me thirty pairs of shoes as well as matching purses, countless dresses, a cashmere coat, good leather boots and gloves, weekly hairdos, manicures, expensive lunches, a four-month trip to Europe and pretty much anything I wanted.

But it was not to last.

Like many others used to being poor and then finally making a little money, I fell deeply into debt. I guess I was not prepared for life in the big city, after all. I told my brother Gus about my debt.

"I'll pay off your Simpsons card as long as you never put anything on credit again!" he said.

I took his advice to heart because the whole incident had shaken me. Over the next year, I concentrated on paying off my debt to Gus. From that experience, I learned to budget my money. If I wanted to travel, I saved the money first. It was a good lesson, one of many I learned in the big city.

Mr. Miles

By now, with two years of office experience, I moved on to a new job, with better pay, working for a chartered accountant—grumpy old Mr. Miles.

"Marie! Get in here as fast as your little feet can carry you. You made a mistake...again! Aaargh!"

Mr. Miles wore a bowler hat and a suit vest with a gold pocket watch that hung from its little pocket. Three tiny black buttons ran up the side of his immaculate white spats. At a towering six-foot-five and weighing in at two hundred and ninety pounds, Mr. Miles was a tyrannical eighty-two-year-old who walked with a supporting rubber-tipped cane.

He bullied and intimidated me at every turn.

At only five feet and weighing one hundred and twenty pounds, I shrivelled under his shadow. But every day I ventured into the ring with Mr. Miles. A staff of thirty had ringside seats.

I scurried into his office, dreading his wrath, my antennae on red alert. He sat fuming, frowning and grimacing, his face contorted into weird shapes. Reclined in his studded, oxblood leather chair, bellied up to his desk, he tugged at his black suspenders over and over again, releasing them with a snapping sound.

"Yes, Mr. Miles. What is it this time?"

Peering over his wire-rimmed readers and banging his cane on the floor, he said, "You made a mistake...again!"

He sprung forward in his chair and picked up his eighteen-inch ruler and bright red pen. He measured the margin on each side of the typed financial statements and the spaces between the columns. "This is all wrong! You're out by two spaces on the left margin."

He angrily scribbled' red X's all over the onionskin paper, scrunched it into a ball, then thrust it into my hand.

"Retype this," he bellowed.

Outraged and seething like a locomotive, he picked the ball of paper back up out of my hand and tore it up right in front of me. Always taught to respect my elders, I did not say one word. But I thought, *You malicious, ignorant pig! How would YOU like it if I scrunched up those single-spaced, fourteen-column balance sheets and rammed them down your belligerent, cantankerous throat...smutty carbon and all!*

In that year alone, I was the eighteenth secretary hired to work alongside him. Some secretaries stayed two weeks, some stayed two days, and several checked in at nine a.m., went for lunch, and never returned. This had been the cycle until I arrived. His secretary of twenty-five years had retired and no one else could measure up.

Every statement had to be typed in triplicate on eleven by seventeen inch, onionskin paper with carbon sheets between each layer. Underlining, done by hand with straight pen and ink, could not be blotched. Losses were shown by pen-dipped red ink set in parenthesis. The hand-scripted covers housing the financial statement were three-hole punched with red ribbon woven through the holes and tied with a tiny, painstaking bow. The covers also had to be underlined in red ink. We had specialized erasers. One end of the rectangular eraser was for the original copy, the other end we used to erase the carbon copies. However, if the naked eye could see that an erasure had taken place, then the statement had to be typed all over again.

At the end of each day, I tried to hide the wastebasket filled with onionskin papers. Mr. Miles caught me one day and called me in.

"Smarten up and do it right!" he told me. He kept me way beyond office hours two or three times a week and without extra pay.

I was twenty-two years old and the most junior among the support staff of four. Doris Ketcheson, a woman of fifty-three, took me under her wing. To help soothe me, Doris mimicked Mr. Miles's actions every time he turned his back. One day as Mr. Miles roared over the intercom for me, Doris sat at her desk, panting in short puffs and beating her hand on the desk.

"Marie, this is all wrong," she exclaimed. "You made a mistake...again! Aaargh!"

Laughing, we didn't hear Mr. Miles approaching us from behind. Disgruntled and just plain nasty, he glared at me and thrust his forefinger in the direction of his office. I followed, pronto!

"You have to work late tonight, probably until midnight," he said.

I recoiled and said, "Okay, but will I get a ride home?"

"You can take a taxi on the company."

At around seven p.m., he said, "It's time for a break. Get your coat. We're going for dinner."

We dined at a posh French restaurant called Le Chaumiere. We perused the menu, then the waiter approached and asked for my order.

"I'll have the New York Strip sirloin," I said.

"No," Mr. Miles exclaimed. "She'll have the poached salmon."

"I don't like salmon," I said.

"Well, you'll like this. Two poached salmon plates," Mr. Miles blurted.

As we waited in silence for dinner to arrive, I looked up at the ceiling and counted the crystals in the chandelier, looked down and counted the small floral patterns in the carpet, then looked around and counted the number of people in the dining room. Not a word transpired between us. Why on earth is he keeping me on when he hardly looks at me, I wondered.

After dinner, the waiter returned with the dessert trolley.

"We'll have the chocolate éclairs and coffee," Mr. Miles said without any hesitation.

We drove back to the office in his fancy new Sedan DeVille Cadillac and worked until midnight. The office had recently moved to a larger space in a new building on University Avenue. Mr. Miles' office adjoined mine. His desk and chair were situated so that he could see every move I made. I felt his eyes bore through my back each working day in that pressure cooker. Whenever I turned my chair to stand up, he would be staring at me.

One day he gave me something urgent to type while a client waited. "Type this as fast as your hot little hands can type."

Minutes later, cruising along at my usual typing speed of eighty words per minute, Mr. Miles loomed over my shoulder and began reading aloud as I anxiously typed.

"Haste makes waste!" he said.

When an inevitable mistake happened, he smugly said, "I told you so; haste makes waste!"

I swallowed my anger. I had stuck it out with this man for two years and he still treated me with bad manners.

That night I moved around restlessly in my bed and fumed myself into a sleepless night full of bouts of tears and frustration. Work brought no joy, only tears. What I really wanted to do was to throw a stapler at him and lock him in the closet or something. Then I remembered my father's words after the bullying bout with Jean-Guy. "Don't let anyone push you around. Stand up for yourself and finish the fight!" So, refusing to tolerate his arrogance and bullying any longer, I made another important decision.

The next morning I marched into the office, draped my coat over the back of my chair, picked up my steno pad and pencil ready to take the usual copious shorthand notes, mustered some courage, and stepped into Mr. Miles's office. I looked him in the eye and said bluntly, "Mr. Miles, I quit. Consider this two weeks' notice."

Completely unruffled by my statement, he said, "What's the matter? Can't take it?"

I controlled the urge to smack him upside the head—right into the next week.

"Take this down," he said. "Put an ad in the *Star* and say, 'Wanted: Secretary. Must have nerves of steel. If you don't have nerves of steel, don't bother applying.'" In the next breath he said, "Frankly, I always thought you looked like a demented little mouse running after me all over the place."

One thing was for certain. Mr. Miles's thoughts were always unedited. They bypassed the inner censor that we all have and went straight into words. During my last two weeks, he did not disturb me in the least. The lid on the pressure cooker was off.

Doris eventually married one of Mr. Miles's wealthy clients. She moved to England and lived in a stunning manor, complete with servants. During a stopover in Toronto on one of her world tours,

Doris visited Mr. Miles in the retirement home on his one-hundredth birthday.

"He's still taking charge and giving the staff there a real hard time," she told me. "He sits in his wheelchair and waves his cane around all the time, hounding everyone. They're all scared of him over there."

Doris and I kept in touch over the years and always had a good laugh at Mr. Miles's expense until her death at the age of ninety-two.

I never expected my next employer's impression of me. I basked in the radiance of his words when he said, "Your great sense of detail and your excellent sense of finish is fantastic."

My strong work ethic carried me through my life, from job to job. It never failed me. I received praise for my skills of detail and organization from every employer after the job with Mr. Miles. Little did I know at the time that Mr. Miles's office had been my on-the-job training ground that would serve me well for years to come. Forty-five years later, I still vividly remember those horrid scenes.

From the left, Louie, Marie, Frank and Vince

519 Euclid Avenue

When I initially moved to Toronto I set out to live with Gus and Jane, but Mike had written a letter asking me if I would reconsider my living arrangement and live with his family because they needed the financial support with the rent.

So I moved in with Mike and Joanne. We moved several times. We did not stay long in one place; maybe six months at a time, then we would move again. Moving around like gypsies was getting old. I had had enough of it, having experienced this all during my formative years. It seemed like Mike and Joanne just could not nest. Mike continued to be a rolling stone until Louie had the fantastic idea that we should all live together. So our final move landed us in a house at 519 Euclid Avenue.

Louie and his wife Caroll and their family lived on the main floor, Mike and his family rented the second floor, Vince, Pat,

Frank and Louie's boyhood friend, Andy D'Aoust, rented a third-floor bedroom, and I rented the dormer bedroom on the third floor next to the boys. Our rooms were separated with a bi-fold door. The boys had two double beds in their room and they slept two in a bed. Andy was from a rather large family as well and had lived on a neighbouring farm when we were kids, so sharing a bed didn't bother him in the least. Andy was very familiar with our family and remained close for many years afterwards.

I started dating a ballroom dance instructor named Charlie.

"I can't take you dancing until you learn to dance well," he told me.

So, when he came over to visit, we rolled back the living room carpet and he gave me ballroom dance lessons. We practised and practised for weeks until I learned to dance, very well.

One night while we were out dancing, the owner of a dance studio located at the end of Euclid Avenue at College Street, asked permission to dance with me.

"I like your style of dancing," he said. "Would you like to teach for me?"

I held him in disbelief. So he walked me over to the table where his wife sat and she confirmed his request.

I visited the studio the following week, watched how all the other instructors taught, and decided that I would like to be part of this. I began taking instruction myself from teachers who came to the studio and taught the hired instructors new dance steps. After a three-month period, the owner of the studio felt confident that I was capable of teaching, and developed a clientele for me. I taught private and group lessons every night of the week so that I could save money to travel.

Some of the instructors would sit on the steps outside the studio at the end of class and chat before heading home. It was on these steps where I first met Al. We had been corresponding for the past year while he was in the navy. He would become my husband and we remain married to this day.

Louie and Caroll sometimes had parties on Saturday evenings. After the boys returned home from their dates, and I returned home from dancing with a group of girlfriends, we often joined the party. When the last guest left, we were still so wound up that it was impossible to turn in. One night, somebody had the brilliant idea of walking down to College Street and having a Coke and fries at the twenty-four-hour Mars Restaurant.

We sat at a table and talked and laughed about the evening's events and what happened to whom. When we returned home we sat out on the porch, talking and laughing until dawn. The front porch became our playground, Louie, Mike, Pat, Vince, Andy, Frank and I joking continuously, and from fantastic nights like this one, deep-seated friendships formed like no others. The nighttime resonance of belly laughter up and down the street did not seem to disturb the neighbours. Surprisingly, they never told us to quiet down.

When we turned in for the night, or the day, the boys' jokes continued and I desperately needed sleep. So I screamed, "Shut up and go to sleep. That's enough!"

It took them a good while to settle down. In spite of my yelling, I was laughing just as hard as they were at the jokes they churned out. It was like living with my siblings all over again at home on the farm. We all lived together in that big white house, and worked by day and played by night.

During the day, we often yelled from the third floor over the banister all the way down to the first floor. "Do you want to go to the Mars for fries and a Coke?" The house buzzed with incessant conversation. There were no secrets.

One Saturday morning, an insurance salesman appeared at the door suggesting we switch life insurance companies. In spite of everyone's refusal, he insisted we switch insurance policies and would not shut up or go away no matter what we said. As a ploy, Andy asked him if he would like a cup of coffee. Four of us went to the kitchen to make the coffee, leaving Lou and Caroll with the salesman. It must have taken us fifteen minutes to prepare because we couldn't stop laughing. The boys stirred the coffee with their fingers after Andy put in two teaspoons of salt.

"Maybe this coffee will get him to leave," Andy said, spilling half of it en route to the living room because he was laughing and shaking so hard.

We shared that house for two years and the fun never stopped. I decided that I had saved enough money from working two jobs and took a four-month trip to Europe with my dear friend, Cecile. I wanted to explore my roots and meet my father's family, including his eight brothers and one sister, but never got the opportunity to meet the sister who lived in northern Italy.

Although we just couldn't get enough of one another, I finally decided that I needed an apartment of my own, and so immediately upon returning home from Europe, I rented a street-level bachelor apartment on Bathurst Street. I truly missed the hustle and bustle of the entire household and all its happenings, not to mention the entrenched friendship we all shared. Those incredible two years overflowed with happy times.

Marie and Pop

Pop

Like many girls, I lived for the approval of my father from an early age, which in my case was not always easily obtained. I always knew, of course, that he loved me, but Pop was a hard man, born to hard times, and he had to be tough to raise twenty-one children. Although a disciplined and rigid timekeeper, he deeply committed his life to his children, even if we did often irritate him. I worked hard to please him. I placed him on a pedestal, and a harsh word from his height would devastate me.

Each morning at the kitchen table, my chin rested on folded arms and with sleep still stuck in my eyes, I watched my father's daily ritual and became lost in rapt admiration.

He shaved every morning at the kitchen table in front of a small, round mirror propped up against his coffee mug. A chipped enamel washbasin filled with steaming water sat next to him. Plunking down in his chair and leaning toward the mirror, he lathered his face with shaving cream from a ceramic mug, then in short, feathery strokes, glided the straight razor down one cheek, then the other cheek, swishing his razor every so often in the basin of cloudy water.

I would stick my finger in the water and he'd say, "Watch it; too hot!"

Then, twisting his mouth this way and that way, he moved the razor under his nose and shaved in tiny downward strokes to his upper lip. Picking up the towel, he wiped the white foam residue from his face. He took his tiny manicure scissors and clipped his thin moustache to the required form, all the while smoothing it down with his forefinger. His tortoise-shell comb, missing several teeth, parted his short dark hair on the left, and then he gracefully moved the hair to the right side as his glinting hazel eyes followed in the mirror.

A little splash of aftershave and he would say, "Ah…I feel like a new man!"

Pop was a charismatic man of average height, perhaps five-foot-nine in stocking feet, with a muscular build borne of a lifetime of hard physical labour. He had a strong jawline and a straight Roman nose.

Pop

He worked as a construction foreman supervising a large crew of labourers. He went to work daily, doing his best to provide for his large, loving family. Always looking sharp and brisk, he headed out each morning with laced-up construction boots, hard-hat under one arm and a metal lunch pail swinging on the other arm. At the end of each day, covered in dirt, he returned home weary, nearly consumed by the dust and dirt and the humidity on scorching-hot summer days.

I overheard people say that he looked like Errol Flynn, but at the time, I did not know who that Hollywood movie star was. In retrospect, I can see the resemblance. He did cut a dashing figure, but I am sure my father's hands were much rougher than Errol Flynn's were!

For special events, Pop wore his brown fedora, with a colourful red feather in the band, tipped slightly over his right eye. A gold-tone time piece filled the right pocket of his button-down vest, the gleaming chain dangling across the buttons. I loved observing him remove the watch with scrutiny, carefully cupping it in his hand, checking the time, snapping it closed, and then slipping it back into the pocket pouch. His delicate handling of the watch— so very different from his daily demeanour—was like watching a bull perfectly navigate a china shop while sipping tea.

I thought he was the most handsome man on earth.

As my father aged and became sick with lung cancer and heart problems, there was a mass exodus of family from Toronto to the Veterans Hospital in Ottawa to see him every weekend. My five brothers and I who lived in Toronto, and sometimes our spouses, travelled the five-hour trip each Friday after work, returning on Sunday evenings to suffer through the week and wonder how much longer our father would be with us.

After six months, the radiation and cobalt treatments were not helping much, and every Sunday night I cried like a baby when I left his side. I went to church on Mondays after work to pray to God to save him.

On Monday, when the priest asked me why I was crying alone in the empty church, I told him, "God isn't able to save my father."

The priest sat me down in one of the pews and counselled me for an hour, but I was inconsolable. I could not imagine life without him.

Two weeks before, his face contorted and writhing in pain in the hospital bed, Pop reached for my hand with surprising strength and pulled me close.

"Keep the family together. Help your brothers and sisters. Help each other as you always have and make sure you stick together."

"Pop, I should get the doctor."

"I promised your mother I would keep you together. Now you must promise me."

"Pop, they won't listen to me," I told him, tears streaming down my face.

"They will listen. Wait and see."

That was not the time to think of such things. I pulled myself away and ran out into the hall and got a doctor.

Those were the last words we shared.

For some reason he had chosen me to keep our family together, to settle arguments, to collect money when one was in need, to provide comfort and solace.

At three a.m., on Tuesday, April 22, 1969, the phone startled me out of a deep sleep. My oldest brother Phil asked to speak with Al, something he had never done before. I handed over the phone and heard my husband speak in hushed tones before returning to bed. I waited until he was ready to speak, dreading what he was about to say.

"Honey, I'm sorry. Pop's dead."

I cried for two hours without stopping. Then I got up, threw a dark dress in a bag that had been packed for six months for the weekly drive to Ottawa, and we left to see my father.

When I viewed my father's body in the coffin, I felt like someone was squeezing my throat; I could not breathe, and so I ran outside for air and cried nonstop again.

Everything was a blur for a long time afterwards.

We expected his death but my siblings and I were still unprepared for the reality of life after Pop. We were thrown off balance and bewildered. He was our rock, our constant. He had been the centre of our lives for so long; it was inconceivable he would no longer be around.

I was furious with him for dying. He was stalwart in loyalty to family, but he had left us. He left me, he left my family, and he left our loving home. We could never go home again for the holidays; Christmas, Easter and all the other events that stabilized the family were to be no more. The twisted grief crippled me. I mourned for him for four years after his death.

About five years after he died, Pop came to me, ghost-like, in the stillness before dawn. He came illuminated, a bright shimmering glow surrounding him. His body was in full form and he wore his fedora with the red feather. I could see right through him. I closed my eyes tight and then opened them, three times, to make certain I was awake. There was no mistaking he was there, hovering at the foot of my bed. I felt peaceful.

"Pop, what are you doing here?" I asked.

"I don't want you to worry about me. Stop worrying," he said. "Everything is okay here. I'm alright."

Then he slowly dematerialized.

Another night, one year later, I sat up abruptly out of my sleep. Even though the humidex that July had soared to a record high, I felt the room become very cold and I sensed a presence. Once again I saw Pop standing at the foot of my bed. And again I could see right through him; he was translucent and a dazzling light framed his body.

"Why are you here, Pop?"

"I don't want you to worry about me. Everything is fine," he repeated. "It's very good here."

And I knew he was right.

His energy was with me. Where I was cynical, I now believed. I was no longer angry with my father for leaving me, because he had not. His spirit was with me then, as it is today.

About six months later, I awoke with the strange sensation again that someone was in the room. My mother, in her green burial dress, sat at my bedside with her hand resting on my knee. She smiled.

"Mom, I'm so glad to see you!" I said. Then she disappeared.

They say that it is someone or something that keeps ghosts coming back among the living. I believe it.

The graves of my mother and father are in a cemetery at Vanier, Ontario, a suburb of Ottawa. My mother's grave was marked only with a tiny ground plaque until 1969 when my father died. Now a large gravestone covers both graves. The inscription reads:

In Loving Memory of Fiorindo Marini, 1898 - 1969
Beloved Husband of
Rose Di Maria, 1913 - 1946.

That tiny dash between the dates of my father's birth and death represents so much more than the passage of time. He was a man who loved his children and whose capacity for hard work was enormous. Despite the hardship and tragedy, Canada was for my father the Promised Land, as well as for hundreds of thousands of other Italian immigrants like him. He came to Canada to escape abject poverty and to fulfill his dreams of a better life. He crossed the ocean's angry waters in steerage, taking almost three weeks to make it under deplorably filthy conditions, and some passengers didn't make it at all.

Pop told us how he was treated when he first came to Canada. He faced deep-seated prejudices. He was stereotyped. He told us people had said that Italians had no work ethic and that they were good for nothing. He also told us that people said his was a different race, from the lowest stratum of the European races. People referred to him as "Wop" or "Dago." But no matter how lowly he was treated or how much racism he faced, Pop found his community. He worked hard and carved out his place in Canadian society. He was one of the Italian immigrants who built the infrastructure of the City of Ottawa. He also fought at the front in World War I and served in World War II for Canada. He was a man of ethics and honour, and the classic strong-willed immigrant.

Pop kept his immigration papers under lock and key inside that steamer trunk in the corner of his bedroom. He revered those papers. He respected the privilege afforded him to come to Canada. Occasionally, he would remove the papers from the trunk, hold them up to us, and point to the document.

"See this? Do you see the paper I'm holding? It means I'm a Canadian citizen. It means I have rights because I've been privileged to come to Canada. This paper is important; don't forget that."

Pop's younger brother, who immigrated to Canada with him, became involved with a criminal group who committed murder after a failed Brinks truck robbery. Because of his brother's young age, instead of being executed, he was imprisoned in Dorchester, New Brunswick. When he lost an eye in the prison quarry, he chose to be repatriated to Italy without a record, instead of finishing his prison term in Canada.

Pop commanded our family, no doubt. Some of my in-laws resented the power he held over us.

"Where does he get off commanding you from his hospital bed?" said my sister-in-law. "Do you *always* have to run the minute he says, 'Come home?' You're married, you know. You don't *have* to do what he says."

Some of them called him "The Godfather." They disliked his thick Italian accent, but most of all they hated the hold that he had on us. They didn't know him. Nor did they see how he held his family together after the death of my mother, how he had taken such care to make sure that we were all fed and clothed and, while he was not educated, he did the best he could for us.

My father always wanted to leave his mark so that people would remember him. If it was a legacy he was after, he couldn't have done any better than with his children. I know my father would have liked the reverence with which we hold his memory.

Pop took care of us as long as he could, and then we took care of him. He believed good families don't just happen; they require discipline, love and fun. He did his best to provide us with those things.

He taught me the power of language and the weight of whispers, and who we are today is a testament to his strength.

When a visitor came to our house one day, Pop proudly waved his arm at us and said with huge pride, "These are all my children."

After our Saturday night jams when we all sang along to his accordion, while we sat around in our usual circle, Pop told us ghost stories about his home in the blue mountains of Abruzzi. He spoke to us of the spirits he had seen, and his firm belief in an afterlife. He tried to scare us before he sent us off to bed, so we would hide under the covers and cling together. He laughed aloud, holding his belly, as we climbed the stairs two at a time, trying to race ahead of each other. I regret that my children didn't know their Italian grandfather with his rough hands, thick Italian accent and Errol Flynn moustache. They could have learned so much from him.

Pop taught me the importance of loyalty and the value of family, and I've tried to pass this on to my own children. It is what he wanted me to do, and in my children's eyes, I can see his love. This is the enduring legacy of my father. We were the sweet fruits of his labour, and yes, we were one big happy family. Everything I have done with my life has been built on his ideal of loyalty and honour to family.

I know of many families who don't even speak to each other except for the effort made at Christmas time. This, to me, doesn't seem like a good time to raise any family issues. You never know when you'll need your family, so don't throw that away on indiscriminate squabbles. In fact, if we had a 1-800-Change-Your-Family phone number, I know of many friends who would be calling us.

Going Home Again

In the fall of 1998, while visiting family in Ottawa, my brother Sam and I drove to Marvelville where we had grown up. I had been feeling a strong emotional connection of late to the old homestead and longed to see it again. Since Sam had the day off work, we ventured out for a day trip.

As we approached Larry Robinson Road, Sam turned to me and asked if I remembered the man for whom the street was named.

"Oh, yes," I answered.

Larry Robinson—the name definitely brought back memories for me. At Marvelville School, my brothers often played hockey with Larry. He later became a famous defenceman for the Montreal Canadiens and was nicknamed "Big Bird" for his size and blond hair. He went on to coach the New Jersey Devils. But back then, although a very good hockey player, he was just another one of our playmates. The road that was named after him leads right up to his farm.

"You know, Sam, a few years back I went to see our old teacher, Mrs. Fader. I felt compelled to find her and found her phone number. She had just turned ninety-two years old when I visited her in her apartment in Ottawa."

"Mrs. Fader!" Sam replied. "I haven't thought of her in years."

"Well, she remembered us. She told me she always loved our family because of the way we stood up for each other. Our 'all-for-one attitude,' she called it.

"Mrs. Fader was excited to see me and we had tea and chatted for hours. She told me, 'You and your brothers really meant a lot to me. I took a deep interest in your family, Marie. You all were such wonderful children. I felt it was my duty to bring all of you up to the proper academic level. I know you have forgiven me for holding you back.'"

Sam and I rode in silence for a bit, the memories drifting through our minds.

"She asked me a million questions and then pulled out her old school files."

"Really?" Sam said. "She still had all that stuff?"

"Sam, she wrote down which years we all attended school and the names of the other students in our grades. And then she showed me a coffee table book about hockey."

"Why did she want you to see that?"

"There was a lot about Larry in the book. He commented in the section of the book about himself that Mrs. Fader was the most memorable teacher he ever had, and then he mentioned our family."

Sam perked up. "What did he say?"

"He said some of the best training he had as a boy was playing hockey against the boys 'in this large Italian family.'"

"Hey, that's us," Sam exclaimed.

"He said he played at recess and lunchtime and you all had some pretty fierce competitive games."

"No kidding," Sam said and slapped his knee. "That's amazing. We all knew he would make it big. He was a tough player."

I looked out the window and watched the late summer fields go by. "Do you remember how we learned to forage for wild herbs and mushrooms in those fields and woods in between Pop's veteran's pension cheques?" I asked Sam. "Pop sure had the ingenuity of making something out of nothing."

"Yeah," he laughed.

Pop could make soups or salads out of almost anything, and he taught us how to identify the flora and fauna and pick out what was safe to eat. Sometimes we gathered huge tubs of dandelion greens to eat when our supplies were low.

Whenever one of us got sick, several of us invariably caught the same bug; it was unavoidable. Sam must have been thinking the same because he said, "Do you remember Pop's old home remedies? Boiled wine with ginger ale and sugar?"

Whenever several of us kids came down with an illness, Pop boiled his homemade wine and sprinkled sugar and ginger ale into the boiling pot. We drank this concoction and wouldn't wake up until the next day, always feeling much better. I smiled at the thought. That seemed to do the trick. Pop's concoction always knocked us out cold.

"That was probably the only time we were quiet," I laughed.

"Must have made Pop happy," Sam said. "It's amazing we survived."

We approached the Marvelville schoolhouse. The sign on the school now read, "Marvelville Community Centre." The bell, with 1924 engraved on it, was still in the belfry. Mrs. Fader had designated bell ringers before and after recess. Each day when school began, girls lined up on one side and boys on the other. After inspection, we ascended the five steps single file into the schoolhouse—no talking allowed.

I jumped out of the car and walked around the building, taking photos from different angles. Sam joined me. I reminded him where the ice rink once stood and where the boys played hockey with Larry Robinson. We peeked through the windows and warm memories flooded me: Mrs. Fader reading serial stories to us; the circuit music teacher giving lessons as the metronome ticked away on top of the piano; a "witchy" black cauldron of soup simmering slowly on the woodstove during freezing winter days, filling the room with enticing aromas.

We finally left and prowled farther up the dirt road and approached what we thought had been our farm. At first, we couldn't find the beginning of the long laneway that led up to the house. We stopped the car and got out, searching the roadside. Then the sun hit a puddle at the side of the road at just the right angle. The water glistened and trickled through the culvert. Pat and I played hide-and-seek so many times when the water was low. Sometimes, when the water was high, we were not able to play there, so we put on a show of tap dancing and singing for our younger siblings. After we rediscovered the culvert, I knew we were home. Grass and weeds covered the opening and it looked so small. As children, we had crawled right through it.

"The driveway's right here," I shouted. Elephant grass and weeds filled the rutted three-hundred-foot-long driveway. We were surprised to see only grass, occupied by chipmunks, squirrels and wild rabbits, where our house had been. Several birds landed nearby, hopping their way across the landscape.

Drinking in the spectacular fall colours, we stood and stared at the tall grass bending in the breeze across the pasture. A sweet smell filled the air, clean and fresh and glorious. I took long deep breaths that immediately felt therapeutic and refreshing, like a cleansing of the soul. We admired the reds, the golds and the rusts of the huge sugar maples that covered the backdrop of the wide-open space. As a kid, I had probably walked this road a thousand times and never noticed the surrounding beauty.

We brushed aside the tall grass and walked right up to the spot where we'd held massive snowball fights, where we made igloos out of snow banks, where we dug trenches and played war, and where we played hockey on the frozen creek using frozen "horse balls" for pucks. I pulled the tips off the grass and rubbed it between my fingers, inhaling the scent as we walked and talked. We touched the old maple trees next to where the house once stood, the ones we tapped with old spigots and rusty pails to collect the sap. Sam and I sat down in the grass and talked for a long time. We spent the day reminiscing, remembering old grudges and lost battles, how we refused to tattle on each other (most times) and old dreams of our future.

And we remembered our father.

Remembering the ramshackle farmhouse nestled among the these sugar maples, I reflected on the cocoon of home so long ago. Through the window of my mind, I saw my family fully engaged in those high-energy performances of song and dance. I saw my father and that twelve-year-old girl I once was, sitting on the sofa, completely enthralled by the gripping arias of Rossini's *Barber of Seville* and Donizetti's *L'Elisir D'amore*.

Sam and I sat silently for a while filled with emotion. So much had been said and yet so much remained unspoken.

Sam's voice snapped me back into the present.

"Right over there is where the old barn used to be. And the house was directly in front of us."

I remembered the dim light thrown by the lantern in an upstairs bedroom and the warm glow it had cast on Nunzio, Mike, Pat, Lou and me as we played cards late into the night, and how we squinted to see the plays and spoke in soft whispers so Pop wouldn't hear us. In my mind's eye, I saw Pop seated at the head of the kitchen table, supervising homework sessions in complete silence as he read his Bible by the oil lamp, his reading glasses perched on the tip of his nose, occasionally glancing over them to ensure silence was being observed.

I saw the clapboard house, the rusty corrugated tin roof, the door coming off its hinges, the rotted steps of the veranda and the broken boards through which someone always fell, the raggedy curtains hanging in the window, and the flypaper that hung from the kitchen ceiling with hundreds of flies stuck to it, some buzzing furiously as they struggled to free themselves.

During lazy summer nights, I relied on the pitter-patter of the rain on the corrugated roof to comfort and lull me to sleep.

"Can you imagine the kids today doing what we did?" I said to Sam. "Sleeping four in a bed to keep warm, hiking one mile and sometimes two miles each way to school, never missing a day even when roads were closed because of the weather?"

Sam just laughed and shook his head.

It was unthinkable.

"We raided apple orchards and chicken coops and went to a one-room schoolhouse. And we shovelled snow from that long driveway."

"Marie, do you remember how we divided up teams to play hockey when the creek froze over?"

I did.

We had played football in the fall, baseball in the summer, and countless other made-up games whenever the mood struck. We always had enough kids for two teams at any given time. Loud, boisterous and competitive, our hidden abilities had shone whenever we heard the words, "I double-dare ya."

Jumping off the barn roof into a haystack may not have been the smartest thing we ever did, but that never stopped us, and afterwards we high-fived each other with irrepressible laughter.

"I don't know if you ever knew about this, Sam, but whenever Nunzio or Mike came home after curfew, they snuck up the ladder and in through my bedroom window."

I recalled how Pop went around locking up everything tight before he went to bed, but after he went to sleep, I got out of bed and unlocked my window for my brothers. When Pop found the ladder hidden behind the bushes, he cracked their heads real good, but he never knew that I had unlocked the window.

At times, when we made noodles and hung them on the clothesline to dry, we dove for cover when company came up the driveway, ashamed of our culture and circumstances.

Sam and I talked for hours, interrupted by fits of exhaustive laughter and increasingly longer periods of thoughtful silence. Remembering that contentment brought calm and tranquility.

I mentally walked from room to room in our old house. I heard the echoes of my brothers' tireless banter after the lights went out. I swept my hand along the bare plaster-cracked walls, tugged and pulled at the handles of the dresser drawer as I checked for "my stuff" that my brothers always hid from me, and hovered over the woodstove rubbing my hands together to keep warm. Home was more than a place to rest from the heat of summer and the cold of winter. It was protection from bullies and the prying eyes of outsiders. A place you could not buy privacy, even if you could afford it. A place of solace and a place of utter chaos. It was home.

I closed my eyes and suddenly I was in my father's room. I found his Bible on the nightstand. His single rosary on the barren wall over his bed hung lopsided, adorned by the remnants of palm leaves from a previous Palm Sunday.

I walked through the fields of my childhood as I brushed the tall grass with my fingers.

Memories of those days massaged me at every turn: echoes of kitchen chatter, playtime screams, my father's fingers plying the keys of his beloved accordion. I saw the warm kitchen with vibrant faces around the table, my father at the head with firelight dancing around the metal frame of his shiny spectacles. I saw my brothers lacing up their skates so they could play hockey with Larry Robinson. I saw my father sitting in front of Mrs. Fader at the school on parent-teacher night, basking in the glow and beaming with pride at her compliments for us. The sounds and the smells and long-dormant images forced my emotions to the surface.

"Do you remember when we tapped these old sugar maples?" Sam said in a whisper.

I nodded.

We roamed the fields of the old homestead and were surprised by the vastness of the area, green grass spread as far as we could see. Taking in the spectacular fall day, we slowly circled where the old house used to be, remembering the hot summers, the bitter winters and the sweet-scented springs. Life had been especially rough in the fall during harvest.

For as long as I can remember, we played together in the fields, building forts in summer and trenches in winter. Long after we had outgrown childhood games, we continued to delight ourselves in frivolous play.

I longed for the past and for what this house once provided—a simpler time with strict rules and order, a time when the landscape was filled with activity. All this echoed to me. Now, without a soul in sight, the landscape looked bare. Although the house was gone, I saw where the structure once stood. Sam and I agreed that we would never see its like again.

As I stood in the empty field where I had not been for more than four decades, I felt a well of loneliness envelop me. A stillness came over me; an ache in my heart. Yet, oddly, these memories lifted me.

How was it possible to feel lonely after living such a life, my days passing quickly with twenty siblings, playing Cowboys and Indians, shooting guns made from odd pieces of wood, bows and arrows formed from twigs and sticks? I live such a busy life now with my own children and grandchildren. Where had the time gone?

I concluded that age is an unfeeling thief. It had snuck up on me in the middle of the night and robbed me of years that could never be recaptured. Before I knew it, I was thirty, then forty, then fifty, then sixty, now....

After a while, we stopped looking over the brooding landscape.

"It's a wonder we all survived," Sam repeated.

'Yes it is," I said.

We both grew quiet once again, and the sky darkened. It was time to go, and having to leave scared me, as if all our memories would be lost if we broke the tenuous bonds to our past.

"Sam, do you remember that one Christmas Eve when Pop charged into the house, shook snow from his heavy army coat as he carried that Salvation Army turkey? We all scuffled to be first to see the thirty-pound bird. Josephine said she should be first since she was the oldest girl at home, but Lou wormed his way to the front. That guy could squirm his way into anything."

"Or out," Sam said with a laugh. "He could weasel because he was wiry and small like a snake in the grass. What a clown!"

We were quiet once more, both of us reflecting on the chaos that bird created when we took turns reaching in and ripping out its innards that thrilled us and delighted us and disgusted us all at the same time. When we sat down to Christmas dinner, we were twenty-one kids fighting over two drumsticks.

That particular Christmas morning we waited at the end of the lane for Steve's old two-door coupe to arrive. We bided the time throwing snowballs at each other.

Gus and Steve in the car with the musical horn.

When we finally spotted his car, we jumped up and down and screamed, "Here he comes! Here he comes!"

Steve brought home Phil and Caroline and Gus and...presents from Santa! Sheer pandemonium erupted. We had so anticipated their arrival.

We ran alongside Steve's car all the way to the house in ankle-deep snow, all arms grabbing inside the rolled-down window to reach the horn. All the way up to the house, we honked the musical horn Steve had installed.

Looking back, the cost of the Christmas gifts didn't matter at all. The feelings and memories that went with the gifts are what have stayed with me all these years. We have all overcome insurmountable hardships through the years, and are connected in ways we will never be with anyone else.

While it is fun making new memories with my family, part of the magic of Christmas for me is remembering the past. The celebrations that shaped my life continue to fill my heart with happy thoughts of home and family. The sights and smells of Christmas at home were simply divine and meal time, the foundation of our home, connected and cemented our family ties.

Even today during the Christmas holidays, I sneak down the stairs in the quiet hour of five in morning just to sit in the silence. With coffee in hand, I look at the sparkle of the tree. The house is very still and my mind travels back home to those days of awe and of warmth.

Having grown up in poverty has left me feeling rich in all the things that really matter: a loving heart, a joyous spirit, a sunny outlook, a loving family, growing up with twenty brothers and sisters with buoyant personalities, knowing who we are and where we came from and being rich in knowing our own self-worth.

We definitely had a rich poor life.

Remembering all this, I knew I couldn't go back home, to my safe place, because without my father, there was no safe place. He was the life force in our house; he made it our home; and he was gone.

Over those many years, it was the family bond that made the hard times bearable and the good times sweet.

After a long silence Sam said, "You wanna go or stay a little longer?"

For a long while, I didn't speak. Memories washed over me all at once: falling asleep to my brothers' breathing, putting homemade noodles on the clothesline, gathering eggs, riding the cows, playing hockey on the frozen creek, falling raindrops on the roof, making the long hike to school each day, doing our homework by the dim light of the oil lantern, singing together by the coal fire, wearing my first new dress, smelling the huge turkey in the tiny oven, and listening to my father's accordion.

It was all gone.

I looked around at the pristine, unspoiled isolation and remembered the serenity of the white-carpeted countryside in the winter, undisturbed by snowploughs or footprints. The wonderful smells of springtime, the long, hazy days of summer, and the harvest of the fall engulfed me.

If time was a river, then my life was rushing past like whitewater. It was joyous and sad and wonderful and achingly beautiful and melancholy all at once.

Home was the place where my soul was nurtured, where we created surroundings that showed a "nesting" feel and displayed who you were and who you wanted to be, and no matter how long or how short a time I stayed away, it had always been good to go home again. Home made me feel warm and cozy and held cherished memories and colourful images. It was a highly regarded place for me, a place of respect and honour.

"Yes," I answered Sam. "It's time to go."

I felt melancholy for a time that was no longer. The house was gone, but home was where it had always been.

Our First Family Reunion

My brother Pat stood up and addressed the entire family during a gathering at my home. His question was something I had often wondered myself.

"Why do we have to wait for another wedding or funeral to get together? Can we not get together *just because?*"

Everyone nodded. Perhaps they too had been wondering the same thing.

"Marie and Al have the perfect spot at their Wasaga Beach cottage. What do you say we have a reunion next year?"

There was a brief pause and I thought about all of us coming together outside the boundaries of an official ceremony. Then cheers and thunderous applause ensued. Pat was the driving force for the family reunion and his brilliant idea was a big hit. It set me on the path to making it all happen.

My brothers and sisters and their families came in droves the following summer. They arrived throughout the day and late into the night. It was a constant stream of hugs and "How are you?" and "How was the drive in?" They came from Sault Ste. Marie, Vancouver, Calgary and Edmonton. They came from Montreal, Ottawa and as far away as Florida.

Heads emerged from car windows as they drove up and hollered greetings. "Hi, Al. How are ya? Can I park in that spot here? When do we eat?"

Al stood at the driveway and orchestrated the parking of campers, Winnebagos and cars pulling trailers. They all found their spots. He directed Steve to the site between the shady trees, waved Mike on to the edge of the woods, and squeezed others into tight spaces around the property.

Nunzio wandered from camp to camp, warmly hugging and kissing everyone. He swept people off their feet and spun them 'round and 'round in one of his notorious back-breaking bear hugs; his victims screamed with delight, and some in pain.

"Nunz, Nunz, you're breaking my back! Let me down!"

Nunzio just laughed.

"We'll arm wrestle later," he said, knowing full well his bear claws would win.

In total, there were one hundred and fifteen of us. By eleven that night, tents, stoves and a bar and buffet had been set up. My brothers and sisters and their families were finally all together at our first-ever family reunion.

The next morning Al and I stood on the deck and banged on a pot with a wooden spoon, quieting the crowd so we could go over the rules.

"No child is to be unsupervised by the water at any time. No one goes in the boat without a life jacket. First one up in the morning starts the coffee. All garbage is bagged and tied. Take care of your cigarette butts. No teenagers drinking on the property—period!"

All my siblings, of course, had been quite used to taking orders since childhood, or at least having been ordered around.

Each night we sat around the crackling bonfire and inhaled the sweet smell of burning cedars as the blue and orange flames danced skyward. Creative storytelling infused the night and fired the imagination of thirty kids as they sat in the inner circle roasting marshmallows. Frank, a seasoned cowboy, captivated the kids with his tales of the west, and he claimed status as a real live "Indian fighter."

"You see these scars on my arms?" he said, pointing out different wounds from his car-racing and his rodeo days when he broke mustangs after wild horse roundups with his Native friends. "The Indians taught me how to make rain, too. Wanna see?"

"Yeah!" the kids all screamed.

Frank and Vince grabbed a blanket at both ends and billowed and flapped the blanket over the fire, smothering the flames, creating smoke, and enthralling the children. Then they danced around the fire and called for rain. The kids watched, awestruck, unaware that thunderstorms had been forecast for the weekend.

There was hardly a moment of silence during the entire five days of the reunion. People were in constant motion and the fun never stopped. As the party wound down each night, giggles and whispers echoed throughout the camp. Snippets of jokes made sleeping difficult, not because anyone was bothered, but because no one wanted to miss anything.

At about four in the morning on the first night, the dark red glow of the campfire smoked and sizzled and hissed as the last person standing smothered it with buckets of water.

In the warm sun the following day, children built sandcastles on the sunlit beach and the adults floated lazily in inner tubes. There were squirt gun fights and football games and kayaking.

Pen and pad above my head, I waded waist-deep into the water to take food orders. "How many pieces of chicken do you want?"

We ate four hundred pieces of chicken, forty pounds of spaghetti, several pots of sauce, six hundred meatballs, forty pounds of spicy sausage, twenty-four dozen eggs, eighteen dozen corn on the cobs, mountains of salad fixings, crates of watermelon and fruit, and a truckload of bread.

The first afternoon, Steve walked up behind Phil and pressed an ice-cold beer in the middle of his bare back.

"You bugger! I'll get you for that!"

From then on, everyone always looked over her or his shoulder for fear of becoming the next target, although since the victim got to keep the cold beer, there was something to be said for acceptance. Some carried helicopter water pistols with whirligigs; others chose the super-duper water guns. Caroline sported oversized Elton John sunglasses with wipers, and Nunzio dispersed white sunhats to everyone. Bolo bat contests, yoyo contests and pasta-eating contests highlighted the week's events, coaxing childhood feelings from each of my fifteen brothers and five sisters.

At the beginning of that summer we had hired Carl, a seventy-four-year-old, retired, prize-winning carpenter from the Czech Republic. He stayed all summer long at the cottage, building kitchen cabinets and applying his famous but secret French-Polish stain. For twelve consecutive weeks, we left Carl each Sunday night and returned the following Friday, and with each passing week we saw that he had clearly lost weight. Each week, he punched a tighter notch in his belt. By the end of the summer, his pants drooped below his hips.

"Carl, are you alright?" we asked.

Carl bought his own food and cooked for himself, except on weekends when we arrived. Then one weekend we finally discovered that Carl didn't know how to use the can opener and was too embarrassed to ask. So, he barely ate anything all week and he didn't know how to cook. If only he had asked us how to use the can opener!

Cautiously, Carl welcomed the huge family presence, but he couldn't escape the devastating bear hugs and crippling handshakes. With each greeting, he took a deep breath and prepared himself. Yet our family still elicited little yelps and yaps from the old man.

One evening he sat down next to me at the campfire and in his thick Czech accent said, "Miss-us...you can't buy this!" He marvelled at the hijinks of the boys. "Never in my life do I see one family like this. So much happy. So much love, Miss-us...you can't buy this!"

As I tucked my six-year-old daughter Michele into bed, the exhausted little girl cried out, "Mommy, when is everyone leaving? I'm tired of all this hugging and kissing."

The reunions became a tradition, and three years later, Michele delighted us with a story written about the family in her catechism class.

"In my family we all eat together and my aunts make sauce," she began. "There is love and peace and joy, and we are all happy just to be together."

In 1995, the immediate family had increased in number to one hundred and twenty-five. We tacked on more days to each gathering, extending the good times.

Nunzio and I spoke of childhood accidents. I related the story to him of having visited my doctor for a checkup during my first pregnancy and upon examining me, the doctor asked, "When did you break your collarbone?"

"I never broke my collarbone," I said.

He examined it again.

"You must have broken it as a young child of four or five because it's very thick and has healed on its own."

Then I remembered falling over the balcony on Booth Street and, in all likelihood, my father probably thought that I had been crying for nothing.

Nunzio told me of the time his doctor checked him out for something and asked him, "When did you break your rib?"

"I never broke my rib," he said.

"You must have broken it as a young child because the rib has healed on its own," he told him. "It healed in a V-formation."

Once we related these stories to one another, Nunzio thought that his broken rib had probably occurred during the times he and Mike piled the rusty bedsprings on top of each other and jumped onto them from the barn roof.

"If we decided to poll all the others, I wonder what gruesome stories they might have to tell us about broken bones and such?" I said to Nunzio. We couldn't stop laughing.

We perfected the art of just being together, like when we were growing up, and I knew that somewhere up there, our dearly departed father was smiling down at all that he had wrought.

Frank

Spirit of the Moose

I need to go to Calgary *now,*" I said to Al. "Frank wants me there to help arrange his funeral."

My younger brother, Frank, had been diagnosed six weeks earlier with untreatable, terminal small-cell lung cancer. In 2001, he was only fifty-seven years old and never stood a chance.

The next morning, before leaving for Calgary, I felt compelled to visit my oldest brother, Phil, in Mount Sinai Hospital. Phil, sixty-nine, had been enduring intensive chemotherapy treatments for liver cancer. The results were dismal. I had been visiting him every day in the hospital for weeks.

"He stands a chance if he has surgery to remove thirty percent of his liver," the doctor had said.

Sixty-five percent of his liver was removed as well as his cancerous gall bladder. Phil appeared optimistic during my visit. He was, hopefully, on the road to recovery. I explained to him that I needed to help Frank with a few things.

"Give him my love and let him know I'm thinking about him," said Phil, unaware of Frankie's condition.

I just smiled and told him I would; there was no need to burden him with the truth when his own condition was questionable. Better for him to think positive and work to get well.

Seeing Frank was a shock. His broken body, half its normal weight, brought tears to my eyes. I kissed his cheek and held his hand; it was all I could do. His neck and shoulder bones visibly protruded. His eyes were sunken and hollow, and his breathing laboured. His defeated face told me he couldn't get through this on his own. The struggle had worn him out.

I couldn't help myself and broke down, weeping by his side. Frank raised a trembling hand and tenderly touched a finger to my lips.

"Don't cry, Marie. You're my strength. I'm counting on you to see me through. I need you."

I swallowed hard and nodded through my tears. His strength and awareness deeply touched me. I wiped my face and looked into his pained eyes. I needed to be steady for him and not allow my emotions to overtake me. Putting on a brave face, I consoled him and showed neither anger nor fear. I had to show only compassion and understanding.

"I'll never leave you, Frankie. I have a chance to take care of the most wonderful brother in the world."

My words restored some light to his sunken eyes. I was glad that I had come. I sat holding his hand, and after some time, his breathing evened out and his grip loosened.

My brother Pat, a minister, had arrived three weeks before me at Frank's request. He needed Pat to take him from a place of fear to a place of peace. Pat's spiritual guidance was a great comfort and helped him prepare for his final days.

Frank called upon me for help in managing the conflict between his loving daughter, Crystal, and his second wife, Teresa.

"Crystal will listen to you," he said. "She loves and admires you."

He spoke to me about his funeral and his need for me to hold things together now. He wanted me to oversee his home and the many family members and friends who wanted to visit.

"Only family," he said. "Teresa can't say no to people."

Frank just wasn't strong enough for the endless streams of people who wanted to see him before he passed away.

"How long can you stay?" he asked.

"I'm here until the end."

"Don't you have to get back to work?"

"I will never leave you, Frankie," I repeated. "Never."

"But what about Al?"

"Al understands completely. He knows I'm here for as long as you need me."

Teresa was uncomfortable about spiritual matters. When Frank and Pat prayed together, it sent her into an absolute rage. She didn't want to hear the word "God" in her house. So Pat and I devised a scheme, a signal I sent by walkie-talkie whenever she left the room where Frank lay dying.

Teresa gave me complete reign over Frank's care and the running of their home. Each day, at ten in the morning, I sent her out and asked her not to return until five. She was too upset all the time.

"You need to de-stress," I told her. "Go have lunch with your friends. Go shopping. Go play bingo."

Teresa didn't argue with me and did as I suggested. But she argued with everyone else. It was all I could do to hold my tongue at her extreme behaviour. She and her friends painted my family with an ugly brush and had no comprehension of family ties. Dealing with her took all my patience and as much diplomacy as I could muster. Much of my time was spent mediating between Teresa and my family and it exhausted me.

I learned how to switch Frank's oxygen tanks, the names and nature of his medications, and the restricted foods he required, which had to be pureed three times daily. Five times a day he had to be given nine different medications. Each meal required up to an hour of encouragement to get him to swallow.

Teresa didn't have the patience to feed him and admitted as much to me on the day I arrived. "That's what I'm here for," I told her. "Just leave everything to me."

She was glad to comply. I obtained a copy of Frank's Personal Directive, a legal document issued by the hospital, naming me as an alternate delegate in the event his wife was "unable or unwilling" to carry out his final wishes.

He wanted to be cremated and his ashes scattered over his favourite fishing spot high in the British Columbian mountains. The spot was a breathtaking, six-hour drive from where he lived on his ranch in Okotoks, outside Calgary.

Frank made me promise that I would scatter his ashes as he wished. "I don't think Teresa will do it," he said.

"I will honour that promise with my life, Frankie."

He was so glad there was someone to handle things for Teresa, who just couldn't cope. I was grateful for the chance to ease his mind during those terrible last days.

Each afternoon for the following several weeks, I stayed by Frankie's side. The sunlight shining through the window on those quiet October afternoons warmed my neck and shoulders as I sat on the loveseat reading.

When everyone was out, I read to him. I read him the stories I had been working on about our childhood on the farm in rural Ontario in the 1940s and 1950s, and the hardships that bound us together. His concentration was limited, so I related the short version of each one.

"It's about time you wrote those stories," he said. "I've been waiting to hear them."

He couldn't close his eyes whether he was awake or asleep; his eyelids were open at all times. He sat in his bed, head back, eyes vacant, mouth agape. The plastic tube from which the oxygen flowed was suspended from a machine near his bed. He woke up every half hour, eyes searching the room for me, hand outstretched, and I jumped up.

"Is there anything I can do for you, brother?"

Frankie always shook his head no. All he sought was the knowledge that I was there. It broke my heart to see his belly wracked with spasms and agony. Scalp massages eased the numbness in his head but I couldn't touch other parts of his body, not even his arms; he was in such severe pain. It was difficult to look at him without tearing up, without my heart breaking, without holding him. At night, I hid my tears in my pillow.

Every time I looked at him, I saw death. Cancer had ravaged him. Death sat at his table and ate his food. When it was finished, it stole his breath. Neither of us could catch our breath, he because of the cancer, me because of my constant tears and my hammering heart. Looking at his anguished face and his look of defeat filled me with grief; there was no escaping it. Three weeks passed and I was as tired as I had ever been.

In his eyes, I could see that he didn't want to die. In spite of his suffering, he still wanted one more precious day of life. It was written all over his face. It showed me the fated route he would take in the path to his heaven. But I wondered, Can he face yet another day of misery and pain?

I covered his cold clammy skin with a towel. He was always wet, as if he had just stepped out of the shower. I told him repeatedly that I loved him, and that one day we would all meet with our parents again.

"You will get to meet our mother, Frankie."

He nodded in agreement and managed to give me a thumbs-up, a gesture that I know took every ounce of strength he had.

I gently wiped a single tear from the corner of his eye. He motioned for Pat and me to hold hands with him, and we climbed onto the bed and stroked his face. He stared ahead without emotion, except when his eyes settled on Pat or me, and then a tiny grin of relief reached his eyes. Several other siblings arrived at intervals during those weeks to see him through his final days.

"Frankie, this is like when we were kids; three or four in a bed, two at the top and two at the bottom. Remember how we all fought to get the dog to keep us warm on those cold nights?"

He grinned and squeezed our hands in acknowledgement.

I saw that he liked hearing me speak about our childhood, and so I began to tell him stories of the old days on the farm.

A simple touch calmed Frank's fear of being alone and the certainty of death. He took great comfort in prayer with Pat at all hours in order to satisfy his insatiable spiritual needs. Just as Pat and I comforted our brother, we found support in each other and in the care of our Frankie.

"As long as he's never left alone, Pat," I said. "He doesn't want to die all alone."

Frank was genuinely sweet-tempered, unlike anyone I had ever known. He forgave his enemies and chalked it up to experience. I remember when one of his friends who wronged him asked to see him one day. Frank immediately excused any wrongdoing by this person without a second thought. It was his second nature to forgive the transgressions of others.

I wondered if Teresa would do the right thing and honour his request. Would I be able to keep peace between his daughter and his second wife? Would Frankie come through this time of fear and find peace with the inevitable? Would all the family arrive in time? Would I be able to honour my promise to him and scatter his ashes on the remote lake miles high in the mountains? Would I be able to convince his wife to honour the funeral that he wanted?

I was a nervous wreck, worried about so many things, and trying desperately to hold it together for Frank's sake. He deserved all that I could give him.

Frank embodied the spirit of the West. He was a rodeo champion many times over, driving cattle, eating by campfire, and sleeping under the stars with his saddle for a pillow. He rounded up wild mustangs and hunted and fished in the mountains with his Native friends from the T'Siu Tina tribe in Alberta. If Frank could do all that, then I could take care of things during his last days the way he wanted.

I took inspiration in his life as I prepared for his death.

Every morning at five o'clock, I crept downstairs through the living room where someone slept on the couch, and tiptoed into the kitchen and started the coffee. Then I stepped out into the chilly hour before dawn, alone with my thoughts. My tears stained the quiet place where I sat each morning, staring into the dark open space. Before long, the faint warmth of the morning sun crept across my face.

Somehow, it relieved me to sit out there with hot coffee in hand, bundled in my robe, a blanket around me to combat the frigid October air. There was something irresistible about the western sky with its grey and purple streaks. A cold breeze, perfumed with tumbleweed, lightly wafted past as I sat on the deck, sipping hot coffee under the early morning light. I heard frantic coyotes calling to each other in the distance, eerie yet mesmerizing. The place engulfed me and confirmed my resolve that a bigger someone out there with tremendous power was looking down on us. But underneath it all, I still felt solemn and alone.

In the predawn darkness, the pain of losing Frank grew stronger. Drawn to the magnificent setting, the openness of the land and the magnitude of nature, I watched the sun chase away the mist and shadows of the night and return blush to the sky. As the night withered away, the sun mounted the hill to drink the dew.

One morning, a great white light twinkled in the distance, subtly changing to a dazzling red-purple sky. I stood up and moved toward the corral and the horses. Out of the dawn, more horses approached for the treats to which they had become accustomed. A lone coyote howled in the distance.

My eyes couldn't focus. In my mind, I watched the sky turn a brilliant blue, and then Frank was there, standing beside his prized palomino, Streaker. He smiled and held out his hand, motioning that he would hoist me onto the magnificent horse. I walked towards him. At that moment Whiskers, the family cat, jumped onto the fence and meowed, so near me that his breath tickled the back of my neck, shaking me out of my daydream. I moved away from the horses and back to the house to replenish my coffee.

Frank stayed in the hospital for his final three days. I wept each day as I saw him waste away and withdraw from life even further. His entire family of brothers and sisters from all parts of Canada were by his side. We all encouraged him to "let go." "Mom and Dad and Lou are waiting for you," we said. You won't be alone."

Crystal and my sister Joyce stood at his side for his final breath, then his body became still. They were struck by his once never-weary eyes that were now closed. I would no longer see his wide mischievous smile.

My beloved Frankie was gone.

It was a blessing when he passed. I cannot erase the images of his last weeks: his dry open mouth, his body a shadow of its former self, the flame of his agony.

Teresa honoured his funeral wishes and consulted me about them. More than two hundred people attended his funeral, including his family, his dear cowboy friends and the Natives whom he hunted and fished with all his adult life. Friends from neighbouring Montana came and paid their final respects.

Many people spoke of his friendship, his bravery, his tenacity. His closest friend, the Chief of the T'Siu Tina, said, "Frank was the only white man I ever knew who shot a buffalo. He was our brother. For his courage on our many trips to the mountains, we named him *Spirit of the Moose*. Our nation did not know one braver than our brother, Frank. He liked to graze danger. He had great power and great fire within. I will miss my brother."

The tributes lasted an hour and a half.

"I can't be alone right now," Nunzio said to me. "I need family with me; I need *you* with me."

So instead of travelling with the rest of my family back to Toronto, I went to Vancouver after the funeral and stayed with Nunzio. But, Phil was asking for me back home. Following my father's death in 1969, Phil had stepped into his shoes. Whenever he spoke, we all paid attention. All of us looked to him for advice. He had become the new "Godfather" of the family.

And so, Nunzio returned to Toronto with me. Al picked us up at the airport and was struck by my appearance. I was drawn and exhausted.

"Let's go straight to the cottage," he said. "You need rest."

But first I needed to see my brothers Phil and Vince. Three weeks before Frank's funeral, our brother Vince, diagnosed with colon cancer, was scheduled for surgery during the week I stayed with Nunzio.

At nine in the morning the following day, I visited Vincent.

Then we went to the hospital to see Phil. I was shocked to see the entire family around his bed.

"Thank God you're here," they said. "We've been trying to reach you. He's been asking for you all night and he's holding on."

But by the time we arrived, Phil had slipped into a coma. I hugged him and told him how much I loved him. He died within minutes of my arrival; so much sorrow, so much loss. It was a tremendously difficult time.

We returned to the hospital to see Vince. Al and I comforted Vince over Frank's and Phil's death.

"Don't feel guilty about not being at the funerals, Vince. It's not your fault. How could you possibly be there when you just had to prep for major surgery yourself?"

We tempered his guilt. We hugged and clung to each other and cried for a long time.

Unprepared for this kind of onslaught—two deaths within two weeks of each other—I thought I would die. It broke my heart. I loved my brothers with all my heart and I could not accept this finality. I was living in a galaxy of confusion.

Back at home, I slept sixteen hours a day and hid away for the following five months, wallowing in sorrow. I no longer saw the world through a kaleidoscope. Instead, I saw it through an empty toilet paper role. The deaths hit us all extremely hard.

But for a dear friend who convinced me to accept a dinner invitation with her, I would still have my head in the sand. In my work, in my play, in my dreams, Frank and Phil stole across my mind. Sometimes I sat sullen and stoop-shouldered in the dark as the room grew cold around me, the memory of my brothers burning in my mind, especially Frank. He was my little brother, and I had been with him in his last, most painful days. Everything reminded me of him. I knew I had to get past my grief, but the loss was unbearable.

Eighteen months later, I returned to Calgary to scatter Frank's ashes. For a year and a half, Teresa had told everyone that she and her own children were going to the mountains with me and she did not want Crystal or Pat to accompany us. She was adamant about this. It hurt me not to have them both by my side, especially since Pat and I took care of Frank, and Crystal was his daughter whom he loved more than life.

When I arrived in Calgary, Teresa met me at the airport and took me to the ranch, where I spent the night. The next morning, she told me she would not go with me to the mountains nor would any of her children.

Teresa had moved on to another relationship and had no interest in personally honouring Frank's final wish.

Inside, I was furious. It perturbed me because I would have arranged for Crystal and Pat to drive with us to the mountains. But it was too late.

I spent the next day and night at a cousin's house in Calgary with Frank's ashes never leaving my side.

Nunzio came from his home in Maple Ridge, B. C., and met me in Calgary. We travelled together for six hours through the mountains, following Frank's fishing buddy, Jim, and his wife Shirley in their car, to the pristine lake. We motored out two miles in a boat to the designated spot and talked about Frankie as we took turns scattering some of his ashes over the water.

We docked and then climbed the mountain. Nunzio and I planted daffodils in the dirt, holding onto tree branches to keep from slipping down the dicey slope. At the top of the mountain, Jim nailed to a tree a plaque that had burnished lettering of Frank's birth and death dates, just as they did in the Old West.

I could tell that this was therapeutic for Jim. Then we skimmed down the mountain, got back into the boat, and ate a picnic lunch that Shirley had packed for all of us, talking of Frank's insane pranks for hours, all the while trawling the lake and throwing back any fish we caught in his honour.

"This one's for you, brother," I said as I tossed a fish back into the lake.

Then each one of us voiced our love to Frank and said our final goodbye as we finished scattering his ashes.

We returned to shore hours later. I inhaled the scent of the tall pines emerging up from the mountain.

No wonder he picked this spot, I thought. *It must be the most beautiful spot on Earth!*

I breathed in the freshness of the lake and caught the glint of shining mica as the sun hit the side of the mountain. I picked up a piece of mica for Crystal as a keepsake of her father's burial ground. After I returned home, I took it to a jeweller and had the mica encased in silver as a necklace.

In terrible grief and feeling overwhelming loss, I asked Nunzio, "How do you feel, Slats, now that it's done?"

"Frank knows we've done him right."

I had to agree.

On the trip back to Calgary, we slowed down for three deer crossing in front of us. They paused and stared at us for a moment. I took this as a sign of Frank's spirit; a sign of acknowledgement of a promise made and kept, and I felt at peace knowing that I had fulfilled his wishes.

I hold a picture of Frank's smiling, devilish face precious in my memory, and through old photos, I refresh that memory whenever the spirit moves me. I take the pictures off the shelf and return them to their rightful place when I am done. When I close my eyes, I can see his face. Sometimes I feel a slight tingling on the back of my neck, as if Frankie is present, watching over my shoulder.

Where Are They Now

Pop and Noreen had five more healthy children after I left home: Jenny, Joyce, the twins Donnie and Ronnie, and my last sibling, Ricky. By the end of 1964, our family totalled twenty-one children. Noreen remained faithful in marriage to my father for twenty-one years until his death.

Two years later, she was remarried to Andre, whom I never got to meet. I was told that on one hot, humid July night, Noreen and Andre had decided to sleep out in the backyard on a blanket in an attempt to cool down. At some point during the night, Andre awoke her and asked if she wanted to go back inside. She complained to him of chest pains and said she wanted to stay outside. During the night, Noreen died of a heart attack.

Although I was saddened by Noreen's death, I did not attend her funeral in the summer of 1978. At the time, I was dealing with the possibility of a therapeutic abortion. I felt my world had exploded. I couldn't think of anything. I couldn't do anything. I lost track of time and cried nonstop for months. Even though my head was in a different space, I should have been there to pay my respects. I'm so sorry I missed Noreen's funeral.

Noreen had been a good stepmother to me and to my siblings, and I will always remember her as a kind and honest woman.

And now we are missing our dear brothers Louie, Frank, Phil, Vince and Mike—and the baby sister we never knew—all cut down too soon. We grieved over the loss of each one. My brothers all died painful deaths from various types of cancer.

Lou died of lung cancer in December 1983 at forty-five years of age in a hospital in Sault Ste. Marie. I'm glad he died surrounded by members of the family. I am told he abruptly sat up in his bed, smiled at Mike, Jo, his best friend who was present, and his wife Caroll, and said, "I love all of you very much." Then he fell back onto his pillow and died. It broke my heart when I heard that. Lou's death happened only three days after my visit with him. The premonition I had when I was fifteen came true. I made a death-bed promise to Lou that if anything should happen to Caroll, Al and I would take in his twelve-year-old son, Leonard.

My sister-in-law, Rita, called me one night in December 2005 and told me that Vince had taken a turn for the worse, and that if I wanted to see him, I should come right away. Al and I had been about to leave for a function. I called and cancelled our attendance and instead we drove straight to Vince's home. In a semi-comatose state, he barely knew we were present. I climbed into his bed and held him. A couple of times during those two hours, he suddenly opened his eyes, looked at me and said, "I love you very much."

After several hours, Rita suggested we go home and rest. Al and I returned home and a couple of hours later, Rita called and said that Vince had succumbed to his colon cancer. We immediately returned to see Vince and said a heart-wrenching goodbye. He was only sixty-two years old.

Mike spent one full year in the hospital with liver cancer and severe diabetes. Within the first four months in the hospital, Mike's legs were amputated. He was delusional most of the time from heavy medications, but during lucid moments, he was as humorous as he had been all his life. At one point the hospital called and told us to come and say our goodbyes. Mike came out of the semi-induced coma and said, "You know, I almost died last night."

A day later I suggested that he let go to be with his brothers and our parents.

"I'm trying but I can't get to the end of the hallway where Pop is standing," he said. "I can't reach him because of all the screaming spirits in the hall. But when I do reach him, I won't have this pain anymore."

Two days later, in September 2007, Mike died at the age of sixty-eight.

They all rest next to Mom in a nurturing place and in the company of saints. I know she is looking after them, finally given the opportunity to provide the love and comfort that was denied to her in life.

Each year on Mother's Day, I honour my mother's memory. She is honoured always, but especially on that day. There is both power and sorrow in being a motherless daughter. My brothers and sisters also felt the weight of life without her. We all struggled with her loss and have missed her greatly.

Anger about my mother's death consumed me years after she died as I came to understand more about the circumstances. I concluded that her death had been completely preventable. She did not have to die and was denied the life she so richly deserved. But through my mother's experience with a backstreet abortion, and the experiences of many other women like her, the lives of future mothers and daughters have been transfigured.

My mother did not live to be surrounded by all her children; she was never to know a single one of her grandchildren. She never got to experience the bittersweet pain of watching her children leave the nest, nor felt the joy of their return. When I became a mother and then a grandmother, I felt the loss more acutely. What I am able to so richly enjoy, she ought to have also enjoyed.

I grieved for myself as much as I grieved for my mother.

Growing up, I had so many questions for my mother, and she wasn't there. We all shared feelings of abandonment and loss. She wasn't present when I needed a shoulder to cry on, a hand to comfort me in my despair, an understanding word when tears flowed. During those times, I wondered if she ever felt the pain flowing out of my heart.

If I could speak to her today, there is nothing I could tell her that she wouldn't already know, but oh, how I would treasure that conversation!

My mother was with us only for a short time, but because she had once lived, I became who I am today: a wife, a mother, and a grandmother. I owe it all to her.

I know she has observed the special rites of passage and celebrations her children have experienced, and I believe she approves of how we all met the challenges of growing up without her.

My mother graces each of her children's homes with her photo in a prominent place. In that photo, she is wearing the olive green dress, her Sunday best that became her burial dress. Two gold-tone broaches clasp the gathers just above the breast on each side. Her hair is pinned with bobby pins; her lips are full and her cheeks rosy.

There is a lot of love and friendship in our family, and we have had more than a generous measure of life's blessings. We grew up in miserable poverty that we called "hard times." Looking back, I see the "hard times" were the glue that kept us together then, and that bind us now.

We all have our own families today, but whenever I am with my brothers and sisters, our spirits rise and our hearts are full. I cherish every moment. We cannot seem to spend enough time together. We are well grounded in family life and are surrounded by everything we will ever need—the sisterhood, the brotherhood.

We are each other's best friends. We make each other laugh until we cry. We share a lifetime of stories. Many heart-to-heart talks keep us inspired. We gather, we connect, and we take strength and comfort in the past, and we love to reminisce about how we grew up. Our memories live and will never be forgotten. We profoundly miss the deceased at each family function. Like my mother and father, they live in our hearts and memories.

I know we have done our parents proud.

I am also proud of my dearly departed father and the very difficult task designated to him in raising us. The hard decision he made to keep us all together, just as he promised our mother he would, has shaped our lives.

I was also blessed with a truly great mother-in-law. Her name was Adele, and with her, I experienced the love between a mother and daughter. I would like to think my own mother sent her to me because she could not be here herself. Adele and my mother would have been good friends. She honoured my mother's memory each Mother's Day during our twenty-seven years together by lighting a candle in church during mass. I loved her for that.

Adele was a truly caring person and the epitome of what a mother should be. She was very loving to her three granddaughters, just as my mother would have been.

I married Adele's only child, her son. What a wonderful man he is! Al comes from a place where women are respected and loved, and loyalty is the rule. He applies this not only to me, but also to our three super daughters, now all young women with families of their own. They, too, are wonderfully kind and generous with loving spirits.

I have always felt absolute love and loyalty from my siblings, and I have given the same unconditional devotion and love beyond imagination to my own family. All this is due to my father and my mother. It is their legacy.

My departed parents and siblings are as real in my memory today as they were in the flesh, loving and beloved forever.

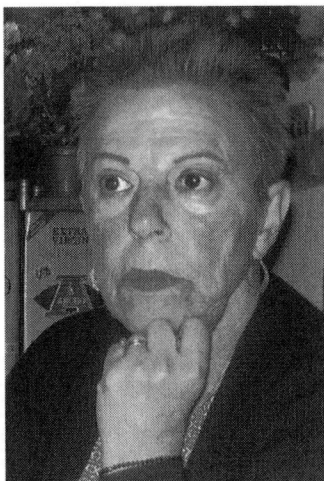

About the Author

M arie Margis has long been engaged in a high-energized life of learning and helping others, especially children.

In her twenties, Marie was a secretary; she also taught ballroom dancing. Working six days a week, she earned enough money to travel Europe for four months and explore her family roots in Italy.

Marie has been joyfully married to her husband Al for forty-seven years and is the mother of three loving, open-minded daughters, Adele, Michele and Samantha, and four grandchildren, with one more on the way. After marriage, Marie decided to be a stay-at-home mother. She taught her children simple math and how to read by age three, which allowed them to go from kindergarten straight into grade two. At the same time, she learned cake decorating and continued to earn an income from her home-based business.

Helping children and teenagers has been a running theme in Marie's life. She and Al fostered forty-one teenagers, many of whom looked to them as their parents and said it was the first time they felt part of a family. Some of their foster children still keep in touch.

Over the years, Marie's volunteerism has been exemplary. The lengthy list of organizations she has worked for includes: the Canadian Centre for Victims of Torture, the Bob Rumball Centre for the Deaf, Meals on Wheels and Amnesty International. Marie taught single mothers on welfare how to budget their money, she learned American Sign Language on her own to work with the deaf, and got involved in the democratic process and became part of numerous political campaigns.

Twenty-three years ago, Marie volunteered for CultureLink, a nonprofit organization dedicated to helping integrate newcomers into Canadian society and become fully independent participants in the community. That led to work with CultureLink for the next twenty-two years in various positions including program manager. She still works one day a week for CultureLink.

In between work and volunteering, Marie learned the art of calligraphy, which helped prepare her for a "Create Your Own Greeting Cards" class she enrolled in. Marie also took watercolour painting classes and, with no prior experience, created beautiful artwork. She engaged in a self-defence course and, at sixty-three, learned to swim.

When Marie wanted to document her family's history, she enrolled in a writing course at George Brown College and learned to write. About her love for literature, Marie writes:

My thirst for reading truly began in Mrs. Fader's class and my love for the classics increased when I attended high school. My father surprised me when he relayed the story of Dickens' Pickwick Papers. I don't know how he came to read such books, but the storytelling interested me a great deal.

About the Author

I often pass my finger along the row of books on the top shelf of the bookcase in my room. That shelf is home to the books I cherish the most. I stare at the Jane Austen titles. The flowery words form a different language used by the refined classes of nineteenth-century England. The language transports me to those times in a slow, roundabout way.

I often remove from their pigeonholes books of poetry by Keats, Robert Burns, Yeats, Shakespeare's Love Sonnets and Elizabeth Barrett-Browning's Sonnets from the Portuguese. In a place of honour reside my beloved St. Martin's Classics, Dickens' A Tale of Two Cities, the Pickwick Papers and David Copperfield, the 1940 edition, and my seventy-five-year-old copy of George Elliot's Silas Marner.

I received Dickens' The Old Curiosity Shop as a stocking stuffer one Christmas. Intended as a token gift from Al, this small, buttery-smooth, leather-bound book with gilded onionskin pages and a fine red ribbon to mark your last reading place, is one of my most cherished classics. Occasionally, I take these books down, along with my high school books of poetry, and dust them, but I could never lend them to anyone. They are simply too precious. It's taken me many years to accumulate my collection of nineteenth-century authors; my books are one of my favourite possessions.

Marie still volunteers, engages in lifelong self-improvement programs, dabbles in numerous hobbies and remains deeply involved in the lives of her grandchildren.

Marie and Al live in Toronto, but can often be found at their cottage on weekends.

99648907R00133

Made in the USA
Columbia, SC
14 July 2018